bullet's adventure: chasing sobekneferu

victoria ray

THE KING OF NO CLUB

Written by Victoria Ray

Proofread by Writing Endeavors®

ISBN 9789198560213

the bridge

. . .

IT WAS JULY 12, 2026.

I stood on the Big Temptation's narrow bridge, the meeting point for the National Meet a Stranger day. A slim woman with curly blonde hair and a floral dress passed by, more or less *flying* past me, only to stop near the handrails. She seemed to be overjoyed to breathe the same air as our passionate crowd, which filled the void of the sleepy bridge this morning.

While I watched her floating steps, I wondered why such a stunning lady would be here, in the middle of it all: the lazy, the vicious, the lustful mayhem, but then I heard her laugh... One part of my body froze, surprised by the tone of her voice; another, refused to let go of her sunny and innocent image. I shook my legs, moving my body below the waist in slow, hopeful circles—warming up strategy for seducing first-rate females. "Okay, everyone, gather around. We haven't got all day, love-birds!" announced a crisp shout behind my back. The crowd squeezed my torso (against my will) towards the ancient short man in khaki shorts. I tried to push his excited face far from my clean purple t-shirt, but the stream of people glued us together.

"I'll get the one with curly hair, a *blondinessa,*" he said.

"The one with the laugh?"

"What laugh? I have the perfect solution," the older man said, chuckling and removing an old chocolate cookie from his pocket.

Thousands of insane images began circulating in my mind. The hungry longing of the middle-aged divorced man, who had failed to become Elon Musk, and who, unfortunately, still had sex with cleaning ladies underneath the stairs of his rented room, twice or less a year.

"No, you can't take her. She is mine, my one and only Sobekneferu Queen." I choked on the last word, realizing the loss.

The old man waved his arms wildly, trying to attract the woman's attention in a floral dress, but she was too busy performing her *non-conversational* skills on the guy with a big beard, gold teeth, and luxury sunglasses.

A slightly bemused female pensioner on my right glanced at my convulsive movements. She became mad as a March Hare, attempting to undress.

"A captive audience," laughed the short man, enjoying his remark.

"Do you mind if we rearrange our places? I'd like to move to the left…" I couldn't finish the phrase because the crowd started to shift closer to the center, cuddling each other in hopes of discovering the dream affair of their life. Hands, open mouths, moans, and cries for help—I glared at the chaos with all fury I had, maneuvering to the lady in a floral dress. To my surprise, she was already flirting with the older man in khaki shorts, who had theatrically presented a thick package of cash from his pocket.

I knew I had to rush. It was now or never.

At that moment, I felt a punch to my left arm. The pain was unbearable. I forced myself to turn and look at the intruder, but another kick sent a shockwave through my spine. I curled up, shouting, "Please, stop!"

A gentle shake woke me up. Two hairy legs, so familiar, surrounded me like a fortress, opening the full view to the curves calling up, guiding my eyes to the hidden grotto of her tight knickers. Each muscle in my body ached; I clambered up onto my knees and kissed *whoever-it-was* with my eyes still shut. Believe it or not, it made me feel half-human again.

"I want you," her husky voice said.

I opened my eyes. "Ah, it is you..."

Her gaze dropped, and she looked at my slightly trembling legs.

"So, do you want it from behind?" I suggested with a soft sigh.

"Behind what?" her eyes shone with fury.

"Calm down, calm down. He is joking. He loves you... He doesn't know it yet. He had too many distractions today, Sobekneferu and such," it was again the old man in khaki shorts.

I watched each of his moves with envy: he was

leaving the bridge with my dream lady—a gorgeous blonde in a floral dress.

"Dammit!" I hissed after they left. "What the fuck do you want from me, Martha? It's Meet a Stranger day, and you are my wife."

"I'm your ex-wife, Bullet."

We stood there for a few seconds, looking hatefully at each other.

"Fair enough," I said, breaking the silence.

When I got back to my apartment, drained from shagging my ex-wife in her rented penthouse, I dropped on the wooden floor of my tiny room, and cried. Between the sobs, I opened a drawer of the antique bedside table: the crumpled picture of Margaret Thatcher smiled at me, sending a promising wave of understanding and pleasure. She helped me so many times, saving me from unhealthy decisions and harmful loneliness… but that wasn't the case today. Without a doubt, I was too exhausted.

"I'm worn out, Margaret. Let's chat tomorrow."

the work

. . .

AT SEVEN AM SHARP, I was fully dressed for my morning adventure on the local bus. I waved goodbye to Margaret's photo and cheerfully ran downstairs, pushing the unwelcome thoughts of reuniting with my ex to the back of my mind. The travel from West, a district where I lived after a nasty divorce, to the train station usually only took twenty-eight minutes.

I have to admit, I loved my daily trips as much as I loved the glowing nature of hot summer, when my body is melting, producing the salty water of acrid thirst. That feeling of being on the bus reminded me about the Thousand Pieces Execution, which once was popular in China. Seeing, touching, breathing the dust of the female hair, watching how the sweat crawling down, slowly, inch by inch, would cut out a tiny square of my soul, bit by bit, until my whole being was slaughtered into 999 pieces.

"I hope you find what you're looking for, whatever

that is," a female voice from under my arm pierced my feet to the floor.

"I wouldn't mind if I'd find you."

"Let me go; this is my stop."

I nodded. The lady leaned against my chest, staring at me.

"Maximus Strong. That's my name." I smiled.

"You already told me that last week, Mister."

My mind began to dehydrate as soon as she left. For the rest of the trip, all I did was pretend to check social media, adding occasional laughs here and there or mirroring the movements of those whom I placed on my list of "wanted ladies."

The bus stopped. I glanced out of the window, accepting July's sunny waves on my skin. Like a bat out of Hell, I sprang to the bridge, counted forty-eight stairs up (as I always did), while embracing the world of trains, the bright spots and silhouettes of hurrying people, then slowly ran down forty-nine stairs from the other side, following the path to the grey building where I worked. The Museum of Archaeology, with artifacts from the prehistory of Rsa and a notable collection of skulls, was located in the brick house covered in moss near a roof that had almost collapsed from decrepitude.

I spent my morning counting containers on the shelves and playing sudoku. At midday, I sat with a cup of tea and a book about Sobekneferu—Egypt's mysterious queen. On the empty block near the book, I started to draw the sign of infinity, thinking about the woman in a floral dress.

I hadn't noticed the boy who was leaning above me, looking with curiosity at the drawing I created.

"I bet you'd like to touch them," the boy suggested.

"That's not what you think. This is a sign of infinity."

"You did a good job, yo!"

"Do you need any help? Who are you? What are you doing here?" I added (as much as I could) the thrill of irritation and annoyance to my questions. And then I saw her, the woman with long dark hair, wearing red joggers and a tight top. I had a feeling I'd seen her recently but couldn't recall *where*.

"Mum, he showed me a picture," the boy said.

"What kind of picture?"

"The parts of a naked woman."

"What the hell is going on, Mister," her eyes slid to my badge. "hm… Harmless?"

She stared at my red face, expecting an answer. Time stopped: a long gap between her top and my desk. A notebook slipped to the floor, making me jump; finally, her fiery steps were outside of my room.

After less than two minutes, my phone rang.

"Would you be so kind as to get up for a short chat?" asked the voice of our director.

"Of course, Mr. Killing." I replied.

When I opened the door and stepped into his arctic room, all my self-respect and self-worth, which radiated this morning, were gone. I stood inside, trying to figure out the director's mood. As far as I could tell, he wasn't a thunderbolt of joy and smiles, rather death and grief.

"Do you know why you are here?" he asked.

I decided to keep it cool and said nothing.

"Do you know who that woman was?"

God, this is boring. I thought to myself.

"It was Missus Vegas."

"Vegas? Which one?" I coughed out the words.

"The fifth of them."

"The fifth? The last wife of Mister Vegas?"

I pictured myself in the coffin, my skull filled with porridge instead of brains, because my brains were on the floor, torn apart by Mr. Vegas's two famous birds.

"Are you okay, Bullet?"

"Not really," I answered, still haunted by the image of my grave.

"Double gin, no tonic?"

"Sure."

I ran to his desk, took a big gulp from a glass, feeling an irrational twinge of guilt. At that moment, Mr. Killing handed me a piece of paper, "Sign here."

"What is it?" My heart sank.

"Parental leave for two weeks."

"I don't have kids."

"You don't know if you have them or not until you give yourself a chance."

I stood outside the room, leaning against the wall and staring at the ceiling. "I'm having a midlife crisis," I said to the space guarding my solitude. Not long ago, I discovered it hurts less when you tell the truth openly and aloud.

What if my whole life was a midlife crisis and that crisis was my only reality?

When I walked past the buzzing train station, some way 'covered' in the chirpy sound of bags, worries, and goodbyes, I felt like the free time of my future vacation was rotting inside of my head, cooking up the perfect food for the worms of fear. I had no idea what I'd do the next day.

the beach

. . .

I COULDN'T EVEN IMAGINE *how the events of the last days would drive me into a corner: at first, there were shining, iridescent meetings filled by the animalistic libido; later, there was a forceful desire to get back to the past.*

I opened my eyes as I felt the cold that emanated from a dark silhouette covering me from the bright rays of the scorching sun. That 'cold' turned out to be a delicious young lady in a red bikini. I sat up, trying to hide my hardened excitement by pulling a second towel over my wet swimming trunks.

"Hello, stranger! Remember me?"

"How could I forget? Sobekneferu of my heart," I whispered.

"Whatcha reading?"

"*Science* magazine!" I nervously scrolled a few pages, hoping to impress.

"I know a very cozy reading area, not so far, in a

cave."

"Gonna be dark there," I said, crushing the magazine with my wet fingers, still not believing my luck.

The woman raised her hands to the sun, dancing in one place, then slowly jumped and, with a few imperceptible movements, untied the upper part of her red bikini. My eyes rolled out of their sockets, the lust for "what could have happened but did not happen on the bridge last Saturday" pushed all reasonable thoughts to the far corner of my head. I growled.

"With this…," she made a twisting motion with her hips, forcing all glorious body parts to play in the wind, with her breasts bouncing up and down like a boat in a storm. "It won't be dark, silly."

Without question, I followed the lady of my dreams, forgetting my clothes, a tote bag, the *Science* magazine, and of course, my brains all in the sand.

On the way to a cave, her Apple watch rang. After a short conversation, she grabbed my hand tighter, dragging me in the opposite direction.

We arrived near the gates of the biggest house on the beach. The master of the house was the famous Flamingo Vegas, the owner of "The Bunny Palace" Hotel and the casino "Sin City."

"Papi, I am here!" Sobekneferu-girl shouted to the odd man with short grey hair.

"Go dress up; we have very important guests this afternoon," he answered.

After she left, I decided to apologize. "Your daughter didn't tell me…"

"What? Magdalena is my future wife. And who are

you? How do you know her?" Mr. Vegas interrupted me, studying my pale body.

"I don't know her --," I replied, the moment she walked in.

"-- It's my brother, Hammer," she announced simultaneously.

"Your brother? He just said he doesn't know you. Am I right?" Mr. Vegas stared at me. My shoulders began to shake, and my head lowered.

"Of course, you are right." I tried to calm him down. "What I meant is I know her. She is my lost sister from my mother's side, but I'd rather I didn't know her, or I should say that I was on the way of *unknowing* her when I met her at the beach today."

"How can you unknow something you already know? Is it contagious?" the old man looked puzzled.

"Aww, don't you see, Papi? My brother is a Vodou man, a real philosopher."

"He doesn't look like a philosopher. What a joke! Mmmm, but you look so ambrosial, my innocent doll." Mr. Vegas put his chubby hand around the young beauty and held her tight. She had changed her bikini to a more eccentric outfit: a transparent top with tight leather shorts.

I felt like a fish washed ashore when I saw two colorful large birds. They were sitting quietly on the sofa.

"My pride and joy! Meet my two best guards: Zen and Dea." The owner of the house noticed a shift in my interest.

"Lovely names."

"Yeah. Zen is always silent like he knows something I don't." Mr. Vegas made a cautious pause. "Dea is short for the Death because she doesn't think much, truly bloody animal."

"What kind of birds they are?" I changed the subject.

"Dodo birds. From Mauritius."

"They don't look like the dodo."

"Have you been in Mauritius, young man?" inquired the furious man with grey hair. "I have two houses there, and each creepy muthafucka on that island knows who Mister Flamingo Vegas is."

"I have no doubt, but I think these birds are Rhinoceros hornbill; they are easily recognized by the horn on top of their beaks."

"You know what, I like free thinkers. I can allow it in my house because you are family, but that's where your free-thinking stops—with my dodo birds and Mauritius. Okay, okay, come here; I'll show you my collection of racing worms."

After the tour, I was left in the living room, surrounded by exotic hungry birds, poisonous insects, odd moths, spiders, and giant snails, each of them observing how I tried to clean up my swimming trunks from the sand.

"What the hell? Are you stalking me? Why are you naked in my living room, Mister Harmless?" hissed a familiar female voice behind me. I silently cursed my director, the beach, and the attempt to get with someone who was not Margaret's photo, my ex-wife, or my pillow. I turned, opened my mouth to explain, facing *the infinity sign* of the fifth Mrs. Vegas. Her body, like a stretched violin string, too close to mine.

"Grab me. Now!" she ordered.

For a moment, we were in another land, far beyond our imagination, but the heavy steps of Mr. Vegas violated the purity of that moment. Ashamed, she ran upstairs, revealing to the world a solid, craving for action, my average Mister Eighth Wonder.

As it turned out, Mrs. Delight (soon-to-be-ex-Vegas) was a gentle soul full of frantic tricks in the field of tantric love. The sound of the waves that day was our music, the French art décor of her bedroom was our tool for wild acrobatic games. After four am, when all the guests had left, when the groans of the magical Sobekneferu had vanished in the salty air, I left the bedroom of the sleeping Mrs. Vegas: I crept to the stairs and quickly walked into the hallway. Something crunched under my foot, but I was too drained to pay attention.

The first day of vacation and the world is already mine! I was proud of myself.

"Hey, sweet brother! Do you still want to read for me?" Magdalena's melodic voice rustled. I was too exhausted to continue the carousel of sexual feasts, so I inhaled as much air as I could and ran out of the beach house.

the crime

. . .

I WAS STILL CLUTCHING my favorite pillow between my legs when I got the feeling that something was wrong. I sensed the air being displaced, the strange excitement in my nerve endings, the wander of breathing in a solid mass of danger, the sound of thunder and lightning—all that passed through me, surprising in its spontaneity. I wanted to believe I was alone, but the flapping of wings over my head convinced me of the opposite.

"We are not here to look at your bare arse; we're here on business," announced Mr. Vegas's shadow, blocking the light from the only window in my apartment. I was well aware that a person of such rank would never visit me without his safety-team, but I'd never imagined that my tiny studio could fit ten fully armed bodyguards.

I hugged the pillow tighter. "What kind of business? You can't just--"

"To investigate the murder in my house. Magdalena convinced me that you are the right man for the job."

"Who was murdered?" I asked again, pulling my boxers on under the supervision of the silent Zen.

"Miss *Amblycorypha Oblongifolia.*"

"Never met her," I sighed in relief.

"She was the gift to the mayor of our city, Mr. Domination."

The Zen suspiciously flew over and sat above my antique drawer where I hid a photo of Margaret Thatcher. To my amazement, Mr. Vegas quickly approached my bed, where I was sitting still half-dressed, and opened the drawer. He poked his shaking finger at the photo of the middle-aged woman, hissing, "Who is she?"

I answered almost unconsciously, quivering from the horror of the situation, "It is my assistant."

"If you find the killer, I'll introduce you to a prettier one. Here's your payment, one-hundred grand."

The fear in my heart dissolved as soon as I heard the number. Mr. Vegas dropped the bag near my shoes, and I nervously pushed it under the bed. The dizzy pinnacle of joy descended upon my soul.

As we walked down the steps, surrounded by the organized army of Mr. Vegas and the demonic bird, we ran into my ex-wife, Martha.

"Where have you been? I waited all night for you, lazy bastard!"

I quickly covered her mouth, and mumbled, "Language!"

The madwoman bit my finger. I pulled my hand away, pinching her cheek in revenge. Mr. Vegas fixed his eyes on mine. Of course, I could tell him that my ex-wife was a cleaning lady, or a delivery woman, or probably an annoying neighbor, but I decided one dead body was enough for today, so I said, "This is my assistant."

"You have more assistants than the stars in the sky. I guess you are an outstanding detective." He glanced at my ex's untidy hair, making his way out from the main entrance. I followed him to his car.

"Margaret is my spiritual assistant, and the one from the stairs is my body assistant," I revealed to Mr. Vegas while sitting in the car with tinted windows. The realization that my ex-wife would find that magical bag of cash tore my soul to pieces, but there was no turning back. I began to cry, closing and unclosing my hands, unsure of what to say or do.

After a short drive, we arrived at the famous beach house.

"Papi! I've missed you," shouted Magdalena from the hall, in tears, with a cigarette between her two fingers. I silently observed how my dreamy Sobekneferu wrapped her legs around Mr. Vegas.

"Your brother Hammer is here. You told me he's the best private investigator in town, and I trust you, lil rabbit," a happy Mr. Vegas replied.

"Yes, he is! A true science man!"

I managed to twist my head away from Sobekneferu's arms—the crowd in white filled the space. One man gave instructions; others fiddled with a magnifying glass near the stairs. I stared at the crime scene in confusion.

"The room is yours," said a man in a white robe, shaking my hand. "I'm a pathologist, Arcadio Hardstone. The body is under transportation, and I'm planning to send you the postmortem report at the end of the day. We have collected all necessary DNA, footprints, smells. I have to add, the victim was pregnant and incrusted in bright yellow diamonds. As you understand, we didn't find any diamonds; someone carefully removed them."

As in a fog, I stared at the pink spot near the broad marble staircases where I was making my way out this early morning. I could hear the bizarre crunch under my foot. Or maybe the carpet was creaky?

"Wait!! Who is the victim?" I stopped the pathologist on the way out.

He explained that somebody killed a rare kind of pink long-winged katydid, called Miss *Amblycorypha Oblongifolia,* who could imitate the voices of eleven different insects.

I was horrified.

Was I a murderer?

At this moment, Magdalena hugged me from behind, licking my ear: "You want to do something later? I'm off after supper."

I raised my hands: my body relaxed and surrendered. I stood in this position for a few seconds, trying to develop a plan to escape her sexual lunacy. Magdalena's arms squeezed me even tighter—her tongue penetrated the weakest corners of my soul. The buzz of the room returned to normal when Mr. Vegas clapped me on the shoulder.

"You can begin, detective. You've got only twenty-four hours to find out the truth."

The process started. As it turned out, last night, Mr. Vegas had invited more than 200 guests to his house, including the mayor of our city, Mr. Domination, and my director, Mr. Killing.

"I can't believe our mayor is breeding them. Why? For money? Science? Pleasure?" I whispered in shock.

"You are such a fool! The first rule of successful investing is to believe. But the second and the most important rule is where to hide the diamonds," smiled Magdalena.

"Hm. Okay, I need a space to investigate, to work." I blushed from the lie and quickly handed the paper with only three names on it to a patronizing face of Mr. Vegas. "Here's the list of people I'd like to talk to."

"No problem."

I was left alone in a room full of vicious insects. I would have liked to become an invisible man... I would have liked to get back to my daily bus-trips, but instead, I pulled out the chair in the middle of the living room and prepared to interrogate my three main suspects.

the investigation

. . .

I WANTED *to bang my head against the door, then growl till I was blue in the face, as I often did in my grandma's house. I remember she said to the neighbors it was a healthy sign in a growing wee boy. Our neighbors prophesied me a great criminal future—the death on the desolate Fleur Moor or in a Mind Disorder York prison. They were too nosy, too provocative, too worried. Thanks to my grandma, a strong lady with a considerable deficit of patience, they were gone from our daily topics, as well as our life.*

I stared at the lonely chair, tugging at my grey suit in anticipation of the meeting with my first suspect. There was an intoxicating sigh in the far corner of the room. I moved towards it when the door opened, and a gloomy man with questioning eyes stepped inside. I breathed in the twilight of his poisonous claustrophobic aura.

"What am I doing on the list, Bullet? Why am I a villain?" Mr. Killing asked.

"I have to admit, I defined my suspects very broadly. Mostly by oversized genitals and with the help of other criminological methods." I felt powerful.

"It was a delightful surprise to see you decided to leave your position at the museum… today. I'd never imagined you were dreaming of working with criminal justice." Mr. Killing said.

His tranquil answer alerted me. Mr. Killing shoved a paper under my nose, demanding a signature. I was shocked—nothing would ever be the same again: busses, books, sudoku-puzzles, dreams about Sobekneferu, infinity drawings—all that would be gone. I dropped to my knees, absorbing the dust on Mr. Killing's shoes. I was ready to beg that narcissistic man to forgive me, but then I caught the sight of a flame, the silhouette full of glitter, the woman with a perfect waist—an image of passion in motion.

I quickly signed the paper and pushed him out of the room.

I turned. She was still there. Her eyes were about to burst out crying, but that didn't stop me from getting steel hard in about five seconds.

"Who are you, angel?" I asked.

"Miss *Amblycorypha Oblongifolia*."

I started to wonder what kind of crime I was investigating if a victim was in front of me.

"Any other details I need to know?"

"I am the daughter of King Hamilton, the ruler of the beautiful land, Gunung Kinabalu."

"Where is it?"

"Not so far away. In Sabah."

I nodded in satisfaction. The princess told me that her mother died when she was fairly young. A couple of years ago, she met Mr. Domination at a local party in Luanda, Angola. They felt a mutual attraction and decided to spend the rest of their lives together. Then she saw his picture in the paper—Mr. Domination was married, with five children. It was a scandalous affair! In the end, her proud father deported Mr. Domination from their happy land. When I asked how she ended up in Rsa, the young woman wept that a vicious Mr. Vegas kidnaped her.

I pictured myself as a prosperous monarch, the first in the generation of Harmless to become a king.

"I can help you," I said with a friendly grin.

"You'd make a great husband." Miss Royalty stretched her curves, opening to my sight a private doorway: her hips were raised to a suitable angle to push my stem into her five inches of deep pearl.

The knock—and the mirage was gone. When I opened my eyes, Arcadio Hardstone sat on the chair in the middle of the room. That dramatic scene had raised some suspicion in my gut because Arcadio looked like a man who'd easily slit the throats of your parents.

"I hate when people are trying to interrupt my afternoons, photoshoots, and erections," explained Mr. Hardstone. "I own The Inner Circle Bank. I don't need any diamonds or rare katydids. In fact, that katydid had a rheumatic heart for years."

"Continue..."

"If you were an outstanding detective...," he raised his voice, "then, you'd know it was the boy. He is the killer! Check a rock twenty meters down the entrance on which sat a red-spotted toad this morning. You'll see what I'm talking about."

I was ready to apologize, when the door opened, and the oddest creature entered the room—a long-haired armadillo.

"My best pal. Gorgeous, isn't she?" Arcadio patted the beast.

"Furiously sexy. What's her name?" I asked, stuttering.

"Jack."

"I thought it was *a female*."

"It is."

"Kinky name. I like it," I lied.

"Be careful with the compliments. Jack can feel when a man looks at a woman with lust and when a man has already committed adultery with her in his heart," Arcadio chuckled.

"Tell her I am not *one of those*."

"Anybody can be *one of those,* especially in this city."

The armadillo bit my finger, showing a sign of distrust.

"Forgive me if I said something offensive, Madame Jack. My English needs improvement." I swallowed my last words. Being there, in a room full of dirty secrets and dangerous reptiles blocked my mind completely. I shut my eyes. Again.

"You are cold," said Miss *Amblycorypha Oblongifolia*.

"On the contrary," I replied.

I felt absorbed by her presence. Before I could resume the eternal conversation about our future, the room turned bright and loud. The annoying boy was here.

"Go away! Haven't you caused enough damage? Never mind the murder and the broken peace of my mind," I shouted.

"It was an accident, Harmless. I had no idea that pink shit was encrusted with some diamonds."

"The best thing you can do is to confess."

We regarded each other in sudden silence. He made a childish *pffff* noise, halfway between a surprise and a laugh.

"No way. You are too dumb to prove it was me!" The boy laughed.

"Okay. Remember, you asked for it." Full of rage, I left the room.

the terrace

. . .

THE LAST SUSPECT on my list was the glorious Mrs. Vegas, but I decided to let things slide because: a) I found my real Sobekneferu-queen, b) my job as a private investigator was done, and c) I had to rush back to secure my money.

I went to inspect the stone Arcadio mentioned because I promised myself to check each clue before announcing the result. Suddenly, I got an overwhelming desire to jump into the sea, to wash away all my troubles, to feel 'simply Harmless' again—here, in this moment, in my beautiful city Rsa. The blazing sun beckoned me to unknown distances; the sea breeze promised to take me to the land of my fantasies; the vast wings of the bird hid the light of the magical Atlantis, surprising my meditational state of mind. In silence, the Zen sat on my shoulder, clawing its oversized beak into my tender flesh. I cried, falling on the sand like an infant. I bounced up frantically, dusting off my suit. My gaze fell on the bizarre pink pollen that the bird had left on my arm.

"What a fool I was!" I wiped my forehead, heading towards the terrace, but Mrs. Vegas blocked the path. To strengthen her dominant position, the fifth lady placed one leg on the edge of my shoulder while her other leg remained in a standing position. She kept looking at me with fiery, longing eyes. I knew I had to go through her intense wilderness with fierce demon-like noise if I wanted to get back to the terrace on time.

"I was hoping we might chat for a few minutes… in my bedchamber upstairs." Said Mrs. Vegas.

I checked my watch, "What for? I know I ought to be over-excited, like previous times, but you see, darling, all I can think of is the crime, the money, and the royal life in Gunung Kinabalu with my real Sobekneferu."

Mrs. Vegas snorted, then kicked me, declaring, "A word of advice for the future. If you are planning to survive in the Vegas world, you'd better make damned sure you are a friend of the noblest and the most generous part of this family."

I had no time to share my views on the matter or to defend myself, but I felt how the local temperature had dropped at least ten degrees cooler than before. I rushed out to the gates, bowing my head in despair. There, I asked a chauffeur in a white uniform to go back to my apartment and bring a photo of Margaret Thatcher from the antique bedside table. Satisfied, I walked back to the beach house.

• • •

It was a warm, unusually bright evening. The terrace outside was crowded, with tables crammed closely in three rows. The middle section was free, with a gold podium. In the distance, I detected the staggering silhouette of my boss, Mr. Killing. I stopped in the doorway, looking at the relaxed Arcadio Hardstone, who was reading a financial magazine.

"Interested in the latest market stock, Mr. Hardstone?" I asked him with a deadly smile, only to tease the ugliest animal I'd ever seen, his armadillo Jack.

The animal raised his fuzzy head, every hair on his back prepared for mortal combat. Noticing that maneuver, I retired into the shadow of the chilly sunless hall.

In the middle row of the terrace, between the tables filled with endless chewing and a cacophony of glasses, sat glamorous Magdalena, enjoying the touch of Mr. Vegas' fingers. She was wearing a mauve bikini. The memories of our last meeting at the beach were still vivid in my mind. I sighed.

"Hey, Vodou Investigator! Are you hiding? Am I right and you know who did it?" Mr. Vegas laughed.

"Your bird is the murderer. Your future wife is a cheater. Your son is a wanker. And your friend, aka pathologist, aka banker is a thief," I muttered from the darkness.

"Only four phrases, and yet such a world they contain," added someone behind my back.

I turned, watching how four guards rolled in something that turned out to be the mayor of our city. He had a round Irish face, creased in a jovial grin that stayed in place regardless of the conversation topic. Each of his guards carried four guns. They looked like men who'd kill quickly, accurately, and passionately. I have never seen Mr. Domination below the belt, and now I understood *why*. Our mayor was chained to a shapeless wheelchair with the help of countless blue pipes. How this ancient man could win over twenty-five other, relatively young and healthy candidates to become the Mayor of Rsa was beyond my understanding.

While I tried to figure out my future strategy for delivering the news about the murderer, Miss Magdalena lurched and unceremoniously sat down near the mayor's knees, dropping her blonde curly head on the blanket that covered his legs. A creep of excitement snuck onto the terrace. At that moment, a chauffeur pushed me out from the shadows, shoving a photo of Margaret into my pocket.

"Please, forgive Mr. Chopper; he is mute and dumb," explained Mr. Vegas.

I envied Mr. Chopper because, unlike me, he did not have to answer to the mighty of this world, working off the money that I may never see. I briskly jumped out into the middle of the podium, holding up a photograph of Margaret Thatcher above my head. The photo was topped with pink marks.

"Here is the proof!" I yelped.

"Closer to the point," Mr. Domination said calmly, narrowing his eyes.

"I would like to express my gratitude to Zen, the bird of our generous host Mr. Flamingo Vegas, as it reminded me that when I placed a bag of money, ahem, I meant payment, under the bed, I noticed pink pollen. A short note: 'I'm highly allergic to any kind of pollen and, in fact, animal hair.'" I paused, hatefully staring at armadillo Jack. "Then, I saw the same dust at the crime scene and on my new suit—the remains of our precious katydid. Let me explain how it all happened...," heart-stopping fear couldn't block my heroic speech.

I openly told to the shocked crowd of high-class beasts how Zen ate a poor katydid, how lewd Magdalena met immoral Arcadio under the stairs, how Mr. Vegas's bored son filmed them, how I left the room of salacious Mrs. Vegas around four am, how each of us tramped on the body of the rare pink creature, unaware of the previous murder, how Arcadio hid diamonds, and at the end, about the evil lies Mr. Domination told to the lovely princess of Gunung Kinabalu. I also mentioned the kidnapping act, performed by Mr. Vegas, who probably tried to help his friend.

"I expected a different verdict from your investigator, Flamingo. Such a waste of time!" Mr. Domination frowned, increasing the cold temperature outside.

Mr. Vegas nervously grabbed me by the collar. "Is this your final word, Hammer?"

His son gripped a bucket of exotic fruits and threw it over Magdalena. Mrs. Vegas stretched her body to stop him but was hauled back by the guards. Mr. Domination was in control of himself amid the chaos. With a royal gesture, he peeled off his warm blanket and hissed to Mr. Killing, "Grab my rifle!" but Mr. Arcadio Hardstone was more alert and agile.

Frozen panic streamed from the sickening air into my nostrils, infiltrating my bloodstream. Without being able to move, I somehow pulled myself closer to the stairs and clutched a stunned Miss *Amblycorypha Oblongifolia's* hand, who was hiding there. After a long kiss, we galloped out of the beach house to the car.

I could hear the sound of the bullets above my head. I could see the swing of the ax and the marks on the doors. One glimpse back was all I needed - I increased my speed.

Inside Flamingo Vega's red jaguar, I crouched down as low as my stiff body would allow, praying to get out from this insane situation alive. Miss *Amblycorypha Oblongifolia's* legs were fully connected to the wheels of the car, but despite that, her left hand went down without any warning and grasped the mysterious object which was climbing out of my trousers.

"Please, not now! Just drive," I groaned.

"Our Kingdom is so fortunate! You are going to be an amazing husband," the woman smiled, watching the wrestling match I had with my zipper.

a never-ending race

. . .

MY SOUL SOARED like a heartless falcon over a wild rabbit, circling nearer and lower to the ground, to the food of its dreams. I looked down. A monstrous horn grew bigger in all possible dimensions, sticking to Miss *Amblycorypha Oblongifolia's* legs eighty-one times, clockwise. After that strength-consuming procedure, she asked me to repeat the same process. I did as I was told because I prefer to maintain the circuits of sensual sufferings until the other half is fully satisfied (just as great kings would do). It seemed the process had achieved the desired effect—patience and perseverance helped me to fly high again. The last triumphant strokes returned my mind to reality.

Miss *Amblycorypha Oblongifolia* pushed my exhausted body to the back seat of the car. She started to drive, searching for a path out of the forest. I sat wild-eyed, surrounded by the thoughts of horror: *what if she stopped and asked for more?* But the trip to my apartment passed without any incidents.

I opened the door, inviting my lady to a calm paradise. A dark curtain seemed to rise before me, and after a second, I could see Arcadio's mysterious biceps, working in a transfixed, quite primitive direction, threatening to kill my peace with his grim passion. My old bed hung on four strong posts with black silk ropes, giving an impression of a small boat. The feeling of emotional terror occupied my being. I clutched Miss *Amblycorypha Oblongifolia's* hand, who shook from the pleasant view of Martha's barely covered breasts, the amorous fragrance of lovemaking, and the resourceful positioning of pillows and little bells, that clinked each time the bed was in action.

"You are quite a craftsman," Miss *Amblycorypha Oblongifolia* noticed.

"Ah, just plugging the Lotus of Phoenix upside down," casually answered Arcadio.

"For God's sake, Martha! What's going on here? And where are my things?" I said, feeling lost.

By *things,* I meant the bag full of cash, but from the shock I couldn't continue, to either shout, frown, or leave. I have to admit, from the moment I saw Mr. Hardstone in my room, I knew I'd never see my money again.

"Things? I invested it, Bullet. In the Phoenix project," replied my ex.

"Ah, I met a Phoenix once; he'd tease the lotus for hours," Miss *Amblycorypha Oblongifolia* sighed.

"I'm prepared to climb that mountain of pleasure as long as you need," answered Arcadio, showing the shortest way to his bed-boat.

"Stop, stop! STOP! I bloody knew it would be like this!" I wept, but Miss *Amblycorypha Oblongifolia* was already on the top of the bed. For the sake of maintaining my royal dignity, I tried to follow her, jumped on it but failed. When I looked up, I heard the voices, which after a minute or two dissolved in the rumbling sound of serious sexual games.

I sat at the table near the window when my gaze flicked to the doorway. There, in the shadows, possessed by primitive animal emotions, stood armadillo Jack, waiting patiently for his boss.

"Don't tell the others, especially my future servants. Ever," I whispered to him.

Soon the monotonous frequencies died out. Without any shame, Arcadio appeared behind me with a peculiar smile and said, while dressing up, "Don't let them guess that you are after their money or position. Behave casually, but make sure your sexual techniques catch their eyes. That will arouse their sense of interest."

I was too tired to think, so I turned, and without giving it a thought, punched him in the chest. He didn't notice.

"I didn't know your name was Bullet," Arcadio laughed.

"Mister Bullet Harmless. And proud of it! The future king of Gunung Kinabalu."

At that moment Miss *Amblycorypha Oblongifolia* coughed, touching my shoulder, "Honey, I invited Arcadio to our kingdom too. He's going to live in the gold house, specially built for those who are so gifted in the art of the bedchamber."

"The unnamed eighty-eight positions are the answer," Arcadio winked at me.

"I've never been outside Rsa," sighed Martha above. I could hear the jealousy in her voice.

"I'll take you, too, if you make a donation to the Hamilton family," the princess of Gunung Kinabalu promised.

I lowered my head and said nothing. I dreamed about my future with my new Sobekneferu. She was flawless; the crown-like part of her upper body guaranteed success and power. We were ready to depart when she pointed to the armadillo. "What about this cute animal?"

"My princess must not worry. Madame Jack will stay here, under the supervision of Martha's mother, right?" I proudly glanced at my stoned ex-wife and curious Mr. Hardstone with the eye of the Master. It was weird, but Arcadio's presence had a strange narcotic effect on Martha—she stood in the middle of the room, half-dressed, in a bewildered wonder, with an anxious smile on her face.

"Okay." Miss *Amblycorypha Oblongifolia* said. She grabbed my hand, and we left the room.

I couldn't remember my time on the plane. Perhaps, we were too tired or asleep. I thought I'd wake up refreshed on the morning of the arrival, but that wasn't the case. Instead, I was chained to an ancient hollow oak tree, which reminded me of the room built like a fortress—a home for all kinds of fungi, bugs, and insects. I was undressed, and my shapeless body was full of nasty red bruises. I was glad though, that my boxers were still on. On the left side, I noticed my ex-wife's fleshy hands. There was no sign of Arcadio around us.

Miss *Amblycorypha Oblongifolia* stood in front of me, with three unknown men covered in bronze—powerful muscles rolled under a skin that gleamed like polished silver. They looked violent in contrast with my Sobekneferu.

"Where's King Hamilton? What's going on, darling?" I blinked.

Her face hardened, and she replied, "I am King Hamilton. Let me explain your duties in my kingdom, Mister Harmless."

the more, the merrier

. . .

HOW DO *you find a way out when you are surrounded by madness? There's no clear answer to this question unless you are prepared for tremendous actions. I wasn't ready.*

Sweet Miss *Amblycorypha Oblongifolia,* the Sobekneferu of my dreams, the one I saved from the dirty paws of Mr. Domination, in the blink of an eye, turned into a formless agamic being called Hamilton. Her sisters' bodies reminded me of Picasso's latest paintings; each time I looked at them, an immense melancholic wave gripped my whole being. Or maybe I missed Margaret Thatcher's smile. She'd know the way out; she'd save me from this horrible reality. Still, the lost photo wasn't my biggest problem. The reason why Hamilton brought me to her country was the war with the neighboring tribe. After the last battle, all her warriors somehow contracted a deadly disease (a syndrome called LKED) that spread at lightning speed. My job was to decipher the letters LKED and to find an antidote within twenty-four days.

"I'm not a doctor," I tried to convince Hamilton's cold eyes.

"I have my own theory about it," she replied.

"Enlighten me," I said as I leaned back against the tree and made an open-handed gesture.

"Relax, Bullet. Enjoy our hospitality and Gunung Kinabalu's fresh air. You are here because I wanted to get your opinion on the situation of my land." Hamilton paused thoughtfully. "Our enemies, the old clan called Beluga, have been sponsored and armed by Mr. Domination in the past two months. Those weapons have killed my father, our precious King Hamilton. My little sisters found him a week ago in a pool of his own blood; his head cracked like an egg."

"Are you quite certain? I mean, is he really dead or is he the Gunung-Kinabalu-kind-of-dead?"

Hamilton took two steps towards me. "What on Earth is wrong with you? He is as dead as he can be. And Gunung Kinabalu is real enough!"

If Sobekneferu could speak, she'd sound like her, I thought. My mind blurred, then went blank. Three bulky Hamilton-ladies silently escorted me to a small mossy raft.

"Welcome to my boat, Mister Harmless. I've prepared some special treats for you and your lady," said the captain of the crumbling structure as he smiled.

The lady he mentioned was dragged to the raft, too, with the help of hand-knitted rope. I found an area on the floor where I could leave Martha in peace and sat near the edge of the floating pontoon, dangling my tired legs into the water. The captain handed me a green pill and a Coke.

"What is it?" I stretched my arm to the sun, checking the pill from all angles.

"Don't worry, it's LSD. You need it if you want to make it to the end of this trip," he giggled. "My name is Captain Happy. I think I've seen you before, boy."

"Sure. Haven't you heard? Hamilton took one look at me and had to have me… as her savior," I joked.

Before our departure, I received a questionnaire to indicate my nationality, draw a family tree, write down my blood type, party affiliation, and sexual inclinations. I was struggling with the list of questions, which consisted of thirty-seven pages written in an unknown language, when Hamilton told me to stop.

"Why? What could be more important than this?" I rustled the sheets of paper in front of her nose. Anger poured over the edges; I was drained of all wit and patience.

"On the way to the Warrior Farm, we are going to pick up significant members of our clan. I hope you'll make a good impression." The beauty patted me on the head and retreated to her gross-looking sisters.

We set sail off the shore. Captain Happy paddled for ten minutes, chanting the mantra in a language I'd never understand; it probably wasn't a language but the song of a drug.

Finally, we made a short stop near the thatched dock. Our first guest was a priest, Father Dionysius. He was a round and awkward man who had bumped into every object on the boat, and in the end, had fallen over my still unconscious ex-wife's body.

"Oh, Lord!" he shouted. "Is it infectious?"

"Why don't you ask the four *Hamiltons* there?" I answered, inspecting him. "As a matter of fact, this is my ex-wife, Martha. I'm unsure about her role in this kingdom, but it seems I am your new doctor. My name is Mister Harmless."

"Our kingdom needs a great strategist, a commander, and a cook. And what do we have? Four neurotic needy girls, one body, and a fake doctor," Father Dionysius replied.

"Do you know what happened to the last doc?" I muttered.

"No, I haven't seen Mr. Sinner in a while," said the priest in a peace-making spirit. "It is not a pleasant task to stay on the Farm. Ah, Jesus would deal with this situation in two seconds!" He rolled up his eyes to the sky, praying and whipping himself with a belt.

I noticed the Bible on the wooden floor—a small book with a brown leather cover. I carefully stroked the surface with one finger to check if it had been made with human skin. On the spine, I read the words 'Motivation and Personality.'

Seeing that I was leafing through the book, Father Dionysius ran to Hamilton and pointed to me as the most hostile, threatening danger in Gunung Kinabalu. Hamilton brushed him off like a bored fly. The offended priest jumped in my direction: his despair reminded me of an unsafe child's behavior.

The raft swayed. We landed on the shore. The man in the Row's navy Nolan suit, crafted from wool herringbone cloth and crispy pressed tapered-leg trousers, stepped on the raft. He had a big suitcase in his hands, stuffed with phones and money.

"Are you a commander or God, himself?" I asked, shocked by his arrival, anxious to beg for a phone call.

"Neither. I am a psychiatrist, Mr. Brahman-Carrado. I'm taking up a free post at the Warrior Farm. Would you like to make an appointment?"

I completely forgot about the priest, but he reminded me of his presence by running in circles around our fashionable young guest. Something flashed in his hand!

"Is that thing loaded?" I asked.

Father Dionysius leveled the gun, made a clumsy move, and pulled the trigger.

"It's a .32 Smith & Wesson," Father said, kissing the barrel of the gun after the shooting. "And there are seventy-two bullets in my backpack."

"What?!" I shouted.

It all happened in slow-motion: I watched how Hamilton disarmed Father Dionysius by using 'the jaguar method,' with which I was quite familiar; I noticed how the three sisters agreed to a free session with Mr. Brahman-Carrado on the other end of the raft; I heard my ex-wife, Martha, who woke up and said her first word (of course, it was a swear word); and I saw how Captain Happy gulped one more LSD pill.

Then I lay down on the deck and closed my eyes.

"We have to pick up a cook… if he is still alive. Does

anyone have any objection to the next stop?" King Hamilton asked, fully satisfied. She shook her hair and gracefully approached my jammed figure. The incredible aura of lust enveloped my small personal space.

"Not at all. The more, the merrier," I exhaled.

the ark

. . .

WHEN ANGRY, *count to four. When very angry, swear.*

My ex-wife, Martha, took the definition of angry to another level. When she realized where she was, she started to swing the raft, madly kicking the wood floor. Three muscular Hamilton sisters pressed Martha's body against the wet boards, but she did not give up. She slipped out from under their fingers, grabbed Mr. Brahman-Carrado's suitcase, and jumped in the water. An angry psychiatrist tried to stop her—it was too late: the raft broke into four parts, and we all ended up in the icy river.

I thought Martha's crazy action would make Captain Happy furious, but I was wrong. He passionately followed her, moving with the waves. Hamilton pulled me to the shore. I tried to grab Martha's hand, but she was not interested in my rescue plan. Later, when our group sat on the sand, Captain Happy tried to explain his reaction to me.

"I felt like I was being welcomed home, as if I had

finally arrived at the place I had searched for my entire life."

I covered my ears, staring into the pitch-black abyss. Martha screamed! I jumped up. A creepy cry was heard from the water: five starving crocodiles tore apart Mr. Dionysius's body. Captain Happy did not seem to notice the disappearance of the priest or the spine-chilling, murderous act of the hungry crocodiles because he continued to whisper in my ear, "I wanted to savor every moment with Martha."

I sighed. *A broken wood fragment, bloody clothes, the loss of a priest and his gun, an empty suitcase*—that's all that remained of our pompous trip.

King Hamilton, followed by her similarly bronzed sisters, gathered the rest of us near the palm.

"Mr. Brahman-Carrado is a traitor! He swam to another side, to the camp of our enemies, the Clan of Beluga."

Captain Happy chuckled, then lowered his head to my shoulder and whispered, "I didn't know how long it had been since Martha had been with a man. By her reaction, it seemed like it may have been a while."

I fell on the sand, stretched my arms, and began to beat myself in the chest, roaring like King Kong. Because of the lack of food, severe anemia, and a complex allergic reaction, only a ridiculous squeak came out of my mouth. Still, it was a joyous squeak because the position helped me to notice the bright light on the hill right above us. I pointed my weak finger at the shiny dot.

"I know, I know... It is the Ark," King Hamilton said

thoughtfully, waving me off. "Hm, it would be better to get out of this place. It is well known for wicked bugs. I don't want you to die, Dr. Harmless."

Hamilton presented her plan: Happy will stay on the riverbank to repair the broken raft. The rest will climb up to ask for help. Martha, probably in shock, expressed a desire to stay and help our captain. I had no strength to argue.

While making my way through the jungle, I dreamed about Margaret Thatcher's smile, a warm bed, and a mug of hot tea. The closer we got to the lights, the more energy I gained. I didn't care anymore, who'd die and who'd live. I wanted to survive myself.

The Ark was carved from solid granite. Its titanic walls weighed many tons; they fit together so tight that it was impossible to insert a knife blade between them even if you tried. Hamilton raised her hand to knock. I took a deep breath to steady my nerves. The doors opened. A slim Barbie-like lady with silky knee-length red hair came out to greet us. "More company? How lovely! Glad to see you again, *Hamiltons*! We didn't expect you so early," the lady faced my trembling figure, and continued, "I'm Ms. Glorious, the local intimacy coach."

Ms. Glorious wore a short dress printed with outsized red flowers, a mischievous smile, and a set of fine breasts. I felt a swell of excitement. My whole body began to melt when I heard a familiar grunt. I turned my head to the sound—gazing straight at me was the exotic-looking armadillo Jack. The devil had the physique of a double box, fat and round, with dyed, pink-colored fur. A disappointed buzz traveled from my mouth. *How was it even possible?!?* While I was suffering, walking through the dense jungles to the place of love and hope, this wicked animal was already here, enjoying every second in the company of the incredibly stunning Ms. Glorious. I heard a polite cough from the left and suddenly realized why Jack was here.

"Glad to see you are still alive, Harmless! How's this magnificent kingdom treating you?" Arcadio Hardstone asked, with a tone of triumph. The man wore a golden cloak that stretched along the dusty road. His whole body was sprinkled with glitter, and two charming giggling girls hung on each side of his arms.

"Meet my sweet company," he winked.

My heart began beating a mile a minute—Arcadio won again! All this time, he was under the safe wing of the Ark, making love to those dazzling creatures, who were, technically, his slaves. King Hamilton looked at the scene with displeasure.

"Enough!" she commanded. "Our raft is broken; we have to spend the night inside."

She ordered the girls to climb down to the river and help our captain so that our sailing could continue without any complications the next day. The girls obeyed, but I noticed discontent in their eyes.

Three Hamilton sisters escorted curious Mr. Hardstone back to the chambers of the Ark. The gates closed, leaving me alone with the bugs under the open sky. I started to bang on the door; my heart was filled with gigantic envy.

"Are you hungry?" asked a female voice.

How could I forget that Ms. Glorious was left outside too! And how could I know that by 'hunger' she meant something completely different—*more mythical, seductive, more grown-up!* Panic began to build in the pit of my stomach, bubbling anxiety about the forthcoming session, where I must perform to the highest level... when all I wanted was a hot mug of tea.

I fell asleep in the morning, still hungry and exhausted. As soon as I closed my eyes, the massive oak door opened, and the four Hamilton sisters ordered us to get ready for the trip back to the river. I was afraid to ask what happened with Mr. Hardstone: he was nowhere to be seen. I quickly hobbled, feeling a fiendish gaze on my spine. Ms. Glorious was unhappy with the outcome of our short relationship. Apparently, she feared the Hamilton sisters more than I feared one more night with her at the steps of the Ark. She let me go.

The trip through the jungle was in silence. When I stepped aboard the repaired raft, the first thing I asked was, "Where's Martha?"

"She is in the box, underwater. I had to place her there to teach her a lesson. She got too angry when the servants arrived from the Ark... We had a wonderful time, though," Captain Happy replied.

When angry, count to four. When very angry, close your eyes and pretend this is the best day of your life! That was precisely what I did, lying on the floor, listening to the waves that carried me along the waters of a nameless river into a bloodcurdling unknown.

no answers

. . .

TWO HOURS of sleeping passed swiftly. I woke up full of boundless radiant energy. I felt like one of Tolkien's heroes, stuck in a fantasy land thousands of miles from home with a war approaching. I stretched out, then stepped cautiously onto the wet surface of the raft and began to cross it, half sliding, moving to a meditative part, where Hamilton was sitting and reading instructions on a bottle of scotch. A real wildfire was gripping my veins; the danger clutched my lungs—I lived on the edge, experiencing the most peculiar vacation ever.

I made a mental note to ask Captain Happy about Martha as soon as I saw him. Meanwhile, I stood in the middle and drunk a twenty-year-old bourbon, which I got during my soft passage near Hamilton. Satisfied, I waited until our next stop: I was too curious to meet a local cook.

On the shore, among the palms and the wild bushes, at first the strange *bag* came into view, then the bone of what seemed to be an arm of our local cook. I waited in a friendly manner to see the whole personality of this invisible creature. To be honest, I was expecting a steaming pot on a massive iron stove and a petite smiling lady with a big spoon. But there was nothing.

The raft cautiously left the shore. I looked at the unmoving shadow with a cute high-bridged nose and blazing downcast eyes, dressed in a hat. That strange being was the famous cook of Gunung Kinabalu.

The hat on her head deserves a special mention in my story: To my surprise, it was made of black plush—a cross between a bucket and elegant feathers—shining in the sun, something that Escrava Isaura, a sweat-hearted white slave, would recommend on GetASAP-Worthy Adviser app if she'd been real. The hat made the woman's head look surreal, dragging my imagination where I wasn't ready to go—to the puzzling, often eclectic novels written by Dave Williams, or probably, to the grotesque, give-me-rum absurdly-hot stories of Victoria Ray.

With a sad, faint expression, the creature in a hat introduced herself, "Hello! Miss Downhill Tasty."

I prayed to God that her exceptional name wasn't the reason for her futuristic, almost geometric shape, her white with blue stripes baby hands, and very casual mahogany-colored hairs on each toe.

I squinted at her as if doing so would bring a larger portion of food on my plate and asked, "So, what's for dinner tonight?"

"Marmalade from algae," she replied, concentrating on her heavy basket, "This is our tribal Grace of Thirty Wounds knife. I got it from my father, who spoke his final word twelve birdsongs ago."

She held a sharp blade, licking the sides of it in slow monotonous torment. I leaned forward and inhaled the strong smell of fish from the basket.

"People have to eat something...I guess healthy marmalade fits perfectly in our daily routine!" I over-enthusiastically declared. "Frankly, I've never heard of marmalade from algae. Some mix of a cement and dead crocodile?"

"Don't insult her cooking abilities, Bullet. At first, she usually washes and soaks the remains of dead Pyrrophyta and Chlorophyta, then cooks it with sugar in open vats, into a liquor, which then thickens into a jelly." Captain Happy gave me a patronizing glance.

I shifted in my corner uncomfortably: my blood sang from the hunger, and the heart craved for new direction in the wild ripples of life. Captain scratched his ribs and laughed, "But you are right, her cooking killed twenty-two warriors last month."

The wind carried his confession direct to Martha's box, which was still dangling under the water. Soon enough, the loop of the breeze returned a low whistling cry, filling the air around us with hatred, impatience, and starvation. It seemed I wasn't alone in my fears.

"If you die," Ms. Downhill Tasty intervened my thoughts, "it will be like being blinded on a sunny day for our kingdom. It'd bring extinction and grief. I'd suggest you wait until we arrive at the Warrior Farm, though. I'll cook a wonderful meal for you, Doctor, from freshly grounded corn crumbs."

I frowned, shocked by her confession, then rose from my place, bent down over the open basket, and grabbed the jelly. I clenched the stolen piece of melting marmalade in my fist, and with a sickening sense of desperation, pitched into wet oblivion.

When I recovered from drowsiness, I found myself tied up to a gold spike in the middle of the raft, with Martha hovering anxiously around my head. She proudly described how she saved me from seventy-eight razor-toothed piranhas, finding my lifeless body hanging on a hook of her box.

"Was there anything edible in my hand?" I asked.

"No," she answered, hiding melancholy in her eyes. She slowly licked her upper lip, which was covered in malachite-alike color, then sighed, "But it was sweeter than at home."

I glanced to my left. The dinner party was in full swing: Captain Happy had fallen asleep, Ms. Tasty stood and stared at the four Hamiltons, who were sitting across her open basket, chewing green marmalade with a rude intensity. Sticky drops of the bizarre meal rolled down to their chins, necks, bellies.

I wanted a bite of it.

Of anything. Just once.

fatal meeting

. . .

WHO KNEW *that writers could be so dangerous?*

Hunger didn't block the flow of my brain activity. On the contrary, it switched on my wit, making my neurons work with increased speed, at full power. It seemed strange that Hamilton had promised the post of cook to Martha, who wouldn't be able to make scrambled eggs even in a conscious state. The extraordinary weakness of Ms. Downhill Tasty couldn't fool me, either. Unless I was kept in darkness…was Ms. Downhill Tasty dying? Was she under pressure to leave the Gunung Kinabalu? Or has she found the love of her life on the other end of this planet and decided to leave Hamilton's clan for good? I doubted it was the last one. On the other hand, you'd think Ms. Downhill Tasty was sincerely fragile, but remembering her remarks about being a master of OKC Marine Combat Knife fighting in the fourth generation, and in addition to that, her knowledge about different kinds of algae, only increased my suspicion.

I shifted my eyes from the sky to the dim waves of Lethe—the river of sorrow and forgetfulness. As Vergil described it in *The Aeneid,* "those who drank of it, forgot their former life and were ready for a new one." Yes, I was ready for a significant change! I had seen the past days' events as an invitation to do a bit of extra digging into my emotional condition and love life situation. If I wanted to evolve and grow as a person, I needed to change my setting, attitude, belief, and strategy. The raft in the middle of nowhere with four kamikaze-spirits, one drug addict, one unhealthy cook, and one ex-wife wasn't the best start to rebuilding myself, but as my father often said, "Don't let the rocky road be a sign of ending; you aren't doomed!" My Queen Sobekneferu was out there, longing to meet me, dreaming of giving me half of her body, soul, and kingdom.

I let out a deep sigh of tiredness when I noticed someone's arms at the far corner—the hand had tried to stop our raft. I shouted to King Hamilton, who had just finished her bedding preparations adapting for a peaceful sleep. Her spicy-hot body bent into an arc, and —whistling and hooting—she threw a spear into the water. Her angry sisters repeated the same operation, but the object continued to cling to the raft.

A strong hand merged into one with a wooden side of the pontoon. Captain Happy made an invisible swing of 'saving' motion, and the body of an unknown man, flying over our heads, landed at the feet of a surprised Ms. Downhill Tasty. Without waiting, she fainted. The rest of our group rushed to the enemy, gathering around him in a circle and examining his pale face.

"You are a doctor. Do something," Hamilton ordered.

"Like what?" I asked.

"Like mouth-to-mouth rescue!"

"Martha is doing wonderful mouth-to-mouth resuscitation. She was a captain of a Big Mouth Liga in our college. She saved me a couple of times, and that's why I married her," I started my explanation, looking around, bewildered, searching for help.

"We don't need to know your whole life story. Please, help this poor man," Ms. Downhill Tasty begged, and then fainted a second time.

While we were fighting about who would save our unexpected catch, Captain Happy bent down and kissed the man. I don't know if it was because of the touch of the jiggling beard or the food resting on the captain's quivering lips, but the man opened his eyes immediately.

"Where am I?" he shouted, shielding his mouth from the drunk smile of Captain Happy, the glowing grin of three sisters guards, who looked overexcited for that time of the night.

"Who are you? What you are doing here, Mister?" asked Martha, leaning against our guest.

"I don't know…I remember I was on a train to Nobel Cave with a tourist group. My name is Alex Raphael. I'm a writer."

"Ha! We don't need *that* here," I chuckled.

King Hamilton hissed at me, holding her finger near

her lips, as she was bewitched by the unusual arrival of that writer, who, beyond dispute, hypnotized her with his enthusiastic stare. I felt abandoned. *Why didn't crocodiles eat him?*

At that moment, Ms. Downhill Tasty squeezed my arm, asking me to pass on a bowl of warm chicken soup.

"I cooked it while you were unconscious, Alex Raphael," she smiled.

I frowned and squeaked angrily. "Someday, I'd love to have a meal like that instead of illusory corn crumbs and yucky fish jelly."

Ms. Downhill Tasty lifted her nose and pretended she didn't hear anything.

When Alex Raphael got up to his feet, supported by Martha on one side and Captain Happy on the other, a crumpled piece of paper fell out of his swimming shorts. I recognized the lovely smile in the shadows of the night.

"My Margaret! Where did you get this picture, Alex?" I cried.

"At the station between Oscar and Grammy. Somebody glued it to the toilet paper roll in the WC room."

"You are lying!"

I grabbed the writer by the hair and dragged him to the golden pole in the middle section of the raft. Seven thrilled figures formed a boxing ring around our two crawling bodies. At first, we tested each other with the help of jabs and jumps. Then, I landed a good blow on the man's ribs, following up with a hook to his jaw, watching how the English writer astutely pulled his head back. *A stupid mistake, mate!* I thought. The audience grew restless, somewhat catcalling. To them, nothing seemed to be happening—we were still alive.

Third-round bell. Still nothing... I sat on the captain's stool, tasting blood in my mouth, touching a cut inside of my cheek. Martha was already in the corner, massaging my sore shoulders. Her irritated voice washed over me like a comforting shower, but I couldn't process a word of what she said.

"It's over! Go to your beds! An equal score, 4:4," Hamilton announced to the thirsty for blood crowd.

To my surprise, all congratulations, gifts, hugs, and even a mature after-feast with Martha, for some reason went to the writer, as a recognition of his latest achievements in the field of Gunung Kinabalu's literature and sports. I trembled, eaten by frustration and jealousy—what if Alex Raphael became Hamilton's favorite? Or a new doctor? Or even worse—a new King?

"Always make a show, don't waste your words," Alex whispered, slapping me on the back.

"Just keep on showing, Alex Raphael, keep on showing," I muttered. Then, I picked a copper spoon from the floor and bit in it, growling through my teeth, "Let me warn you, Mister Writer, sometimes showing all the details can spoil the end result of the story."

He pretended to think for a moment, "Can't wait to see that ending, Bullet. Let's hope it turns out well for you..."

screw quarter

. . .

I WELCOMED *the first rays of sun with enthusiastic cheer. After a long trip—full of obstacles, spiritual slumber, and excessive heat—I felt like a bear, awake and moving in the direction of the dawning light.*

We arrived at the east riverbank of Gunung Kinabalu, closer to the lunch. Three cars, one of which was a beautiful Bentley R-Type Continental from 1952, were already waiting for us. The second car, a Buick Roadmaster Skylark, had flowers and fruit carved on each side of the doors: it gleamed with a deep red light. All I could think of was how much I'd like to slide inside that Buick, to be carried away from Hamilton's madness, from my new professional responsibilities, somewhere far away, to a stylish house with a proper bath and, of course, a bedroom with crispy Egyptian sheets.

Near the third car, a Model V Stuffy, an electric giant of 21st century, stood a sunburnt Arcadio. He was dressed in an ivory-colored linen shirt, beige beach trousers, and a wide, welcoming smile. He ran down to our tired procession, put his strong arm around King Hamilton's waist, and tried to steer her to his car.

"My darling, all is arranged for your arrival," said Arcadio Hardstone.

Then, he barked something to her three sisters, who didn't look very pleased by his order, but did what they'd been told: they tied Martha and me to the roof of grey Bentley. Lucky Ms. Downhill Tasty got a spare place inside, between two soft pillows, where the famous armadillo Jack already snored.

To my surprise, the driver of our vehicle was Ms. Glorious. She was dressed in blue swimming shorts with a yellow kaftan. The other lady near her was wrapped in a green towel and looked like an angry mosquito. The third woman, who sat at the back, glanced coldly at me; she held a bulk sketchbook, a pencil, and a phone in her hands.

"Are you ready for some whoopee-trip, Dr. Harmless?" Ms. Glorious knocked on the ceiling and started the engine.

Our destination, the so-called 'Warrior Farm,' was seventeen miles away. The road was bumpy and dusty; the sky was too dazzling to look at, turning from turquoise to pink, from yellow to red. The closer we came to the farm, the noisier our environment grew. Ginger-colored exotic birds— silent, hateful, persistent —followed our journey on the sandy track. Finally, the road ended abruptly: the cars stopped near the narrow tunnel with a golden gate—the entrance into the green hill where the famous town of Gunung Kinabalu was hidden.

After our arrival, the crowd's eyes inspected my aching body and face, covered in rolls of insects, the tissue of luxurious cigarettes, brown fur, and orange feathers in various sizes. Ms. Glorious, covering her mouth with her hand, chuckled, "What has happened to you, Doc?"

"I fell from the roof... a couple of times. Martha helped me up, though. Nothing to worry about."

Life is not fair: I dreamed of impressing the ladies of the Warrior Farm, but I failed, again.

The place was surprisingly modern: tall towers, polished streets with electric lamps and vehicles, soft music from balconies and laughter at the steps of the bar—the rhythm of civilization, so different from what I'd experienced during the past week. Warrior Farm was a vast, unpredictable, grand town in the middle of nowhere.

The woman with a sheriff's badge hugged me without any introduction. I stopped breathing: she could easily have been the most beautiful sheriff I'd ever seen—on the screen or in reality—dressed in a silky purple kimono with an ample décolletage.

"I can't believe this is the man who is going to cure eleven thousand of our sick warriors! Does he know anything about the dangerous virus LKED? He looks like a rat," the women in the crowd whispered.

"Rat? I beg your pardon!" I turned around, trying to find the offender between unfamiliar faces.

"They might mean the guinea pig," Ms. Downhill Tasty giggled.

The group dissolved: some women went to the saloon, others to the hairdresser, bar, or spa. They didn't look too sick. My eyes traveled with satisfaction around this little perfect kingdom. I breathed in all the sounds and smells of the Warrior Land, convincing myself that this is the place I was meant to be now, at this precise moment of my life.

The gentle jolt on my back woke me up from my deep thoughts.

"There's a party on the Dope yacht tonight, to celebrate your arrival at Screw Quarter," the stunning sheriff informed me.

"Screw Quarter? I thought this is a Warrior Farm," I blinked.

"Honey, Warrior Farm is seven miles away, behind thirty meters high, steel walls, surrounded by the cold river from one side and the deadly forest from the other. Your lovely, but mad, patients are locked in there," sheriff paused to make a sickening clicking sound. "And tomorrow, you'll be delivered inside, together with your cook Martha for a closer inspection and, hopefully, the right diagnosis and careful treatment. You'll find the necessary weapons and new clothes in the room above Death-Watch Tower, in far south of Screw Quarter, behind the drug store of Ms. Sedative."

"Weapons? I'm a doctor!" I shouted.

"Well, Warrior Farm is a dangerous place. Every night there is more and more violence," sheriff instinctively dropped her voice and leaned closer.

"What kind of violence?"

The widening eyes of the sheriff and the fluffy rings from her luxury cigarette said that all.

"Can I use a phone? I saw a phone in the car during the trip to Screw Quarter," I begged.

"Ah, that... sure, but it doesn't work. Only Beluga Clan has a direct satellite connection, and they rarely share access with us. We are in the middle of a war, as you know... I heard your friend, Arcadio, is trying to negotiate better terms."

The realization of my current situation came as a shock. I went to the saloon, slowly moving my wadded feet to the stimulating drug of *whatever was served*.

one percent

. . .

I SAT at the maple table and listened to the conversations at the bar. Despite increasing attention and distrust of the saloon's regulars, I found out that roughly one percent of Gunung Kinabalu owned ninety-two percent of the kingdom's wealth. The gap between the high-tech quarter and the rest of the land widened last year. Constant taxes, erosion of farmers' rights, cost-cutting, and systematic inequality created the perfect conditions for the first wave of resistance. Strangely enough, the wealthy part of the population named it 'LKED-virus.' It seemed, the sweet geniality of Screw Quarter, where fewer than a hundred female citizens lived, was pure deception.

I drank more, enjoying the bitter conversation between three older ladies: at first about warriors who "always painted the wrong picture of life," later about farmers who "were obsessed with the style of living in the Screw area rather than shutting up and working for their king."

I tried to take a leading part in their conversation and explain that Hamilton could reduce taxes, increase competition, enforce liberal reforms, and change property rights, but the sheriff's arrival stopped my poignant speech. She ordered a 'Forget Your Identity' cocktail and shared with me the sad story of Mr. Sinner, a previous doctor, who had been treated as a missing person for the past three weeks. Unfortunately, her hopes of finding him alive were fading away with each hour.

"We don't give up, though. We are planning to continue our hunt with the help of new Full Screw technology," she winked. After that remark, I drained a full glass of vodka in seconds, then referred to my lack of knowledge of the matter and left the saloon.

I was standing outside, watching the swarms of insects passing by, when my interest was attracted by a strange movement behind the church. The shadow of charming Ms. Glorious separated from the walls. I instinctively stepped back, hiding under the tree, suddenly feeling sober.

"Shall we resume our last conversation in my private 'Be Very Afraid' penthouse?" Ms. Glorious asked, darting holes in my bare chest.

"Another time. I know it's very upsetting, considering all those memories we shared outside of the Ark, but...," I mumbled, stretching my elastic shorts up and down, previously delivered by Hamilton's sister to the saloon and cursing the unforgiving heat.

"Ah, stop it, you'll destroy the fabric! These shorts are made from organic thyme-fragrant lace and ordered directly from Paris."

"I'm being eaten alive by the bugs... Can I borrow your kimono for tonight?" I asked, ashamed of how little I knew about the fashion in her country.

"It isn't legal in Screw Quarter, Harmless," added Arcadio Hardstone. "Kimonos are only for citizens. And you aren't one yet."

He stepped out from the darkness; his angry eyes fixed on my awkward movements. Ms. Glorious became speechless, then she admirably nodded to Arcadio and disappeared into the shadows, far beyond my reach.

A heavy silence invaded the air. Without any warning, Arcadio pushed me to the tree and brought his knee as hard as he could into my groin.

"Who are you working for?" He asked.

"I don't understand what you mean," I cried.

"You've got no protection here, slop. We've already killed one of your 999-agents, known to the authorities as Dr. Sinner. Do you want to be the next?"

"This is ridiculous! You know me, Arcadio. I'm an archaeologist! I grew up in Rsa, and I lived there my whole life!"

"Hm. Then you won't object to a body search, just in case you are hiding a secret weapon inside of your shorts."

"What for? You can see through them!"

The conversation didn't last more than a few

minutes, but I felt that the entire scene was just an excuse.

"Wait," I whispered, changing my tactic. "Not in front of the church and saloon. Too many eyes." I flushed, inviting Arcadio into the dark alley that led to the bright swimming pool area. He obeyed, graciously following me to the lights. To my relief, someone was already there. The lonely swimmer was none other than Martha, naked and entirely unaware we were watching her every move. She looked so sweet, optimistic, and friendly—almost happy.

Martha dived in, automatically bringing our attention to the usually invisible parts of her body.

"Jump in! I'll take care of you both," she laughed.

I began to explain how tired I was, how heat burned my hands, and that sharp pain shot through them with each thought. I was standing there, as the holiest of saints, unable to stop shaking, babbling empty words, surrounded by the glowing light from the pool, while the world around me was falling apart.

"Serve me your inestimable love!" Martha howled.

The ground beneath my body swallowed me up. After quivering a minute, I finally opened my mouth to finish my pointless explanation but noticed that Arcadio had already jumped into the pool. I watched how his marvelous shoulders moved towards Martha, promptly surrounding her with his icy-cold, domineering, unyielding embrace. He pulled her legs over his arms, lightly pressing my usually strong ex-wife to the corner of the pool, then turned his head and smiled.

That smile unsettled me somehow: Arcadio was yet a mystery to me.

Gradually, my full awareness returned. I sighed, took a plate of freshly chopped ananas chips, and poured a glass of champagne from the opened bottle of Louis Roederer Cristal Brut, 2008. Then, quietly, without breathing, I lay down on the deck chair, enjoying the sound of passion pounding out of the pool.

"It's so funny, but I *see* us both—*you and me*—in the other corner of the pool," the sheriff murmured behind me.

Of course, I made an effort to decline her mad fantasy while melting under the passionate gaze of her grey eyes. I didn't succeed. **Well, you don't need my help to imagine the rest...**

miss sedative & co

. . .

THE FOUR OF us sat outside on the pool terrace, with a mojito in hand, desperately trying to find a common topic for conversation.

"Arcadio, where did you learn to create such a high wave of sexual latitudes? It was quite incredible," Martha asked.

"Just following the wind, sweetheart," he grinned.

The high-security guard of the pool area, the armadillo Jack, walked past me and crammed himself into a small box (that looked like a coffin) under the terrace table. He was utterly exhausted. Watching him suffer made me happy.

It was weird being surrounded by the two people I disliked the most, but the energy around me, the cloud of secretiveness, made me stay. I wanted to know more about the Gunung Kinabalu Kingdom, Screw Quarter universe, and how it all worked. I hoped that the hot-tempered games in the pool were the way to find out the answer.

I don't know how long we lay there, drained out of all strength. I heard the clumped steps and turned my head to the sound. With a silver bell on his foot, a peacock of exceptional beauty came out of the darkness, blocking the moonlight. Armadillo Jack jerked up and headed towards it. The peacock didn't look very surprised, so I assumed that they had met before.

I was still chewing the last ice cubes from my mojito when the sheriff, who hadn't said a word after our dynamic swim in the pool, stood up and announced, "I was impressed by your *brush*, Dr. Harmless. But I must ask you to visit the intimate saloon of Ms. Wicked-Breaker, to have a professional cut for our next close-up session."

Arcadio stared at me like I'd grown a second penis. I felt confused and anxious; my face flashed in all possible nuances of red.

"Such a pity we don't have enough time to re-group our positions. Hopefully, we'll continue at the Dope party," she added.

I was shocked by her comment: the blood under my skin raised to the level of rapid simmer. One more nasty mention would make my heart explode. Seeing my erratic convulsions, sheriff patted my wet hair, leaned closer, and whispered, "I must confess, just the look of it terrified me. I have unusually sensitive skin, too."

"About time," laughed Martha. "I told you when we first met. If you'd listened, you'd have saved yourself from heartache, Bullet."

The sheriff left our company, but her mean note was

playing on repeat in my head as a roar of bitterness and fury.

The rays of light peeked out from the East, and the Screw Quarter woke up to life. Arcadio proposed to help me to get safely to the house of Ms. Sedative. I tried to convince him that I was the best in the orientation class in college and asked him to draw me a map of the Death Tower, but he declined. I felt like a bull harnessed to a cart, with a cabman holding a whip behind my back: what could be worse than that? From the other side, I knew I'd never find the road to the Death Tower on my own. Not in these crazy jungles of the femme fatale population.

We made our way through the streets, drowning in the sounds of shouting women about champagne baths, belly dance lessons, triple nails painting, and emerald-green eye patches for the wrinkles. The closer we got to the Death Tower of the mysterious Ms. Sedative, the more the rhythm of the streets changed: the voices became more profound, heavier, full of dreamless, esoteric moans, and weirdly shaped, extravagant, masquerade costumes.

Ms. Sedative's house was a plantation-style villa with a small white citadel on the top floor. Four pavilions embraced a lengthy pool, designed in Ralph York's Caribbean style with cushioned rattan chairs, maritime art, hurricane lamps, and a vast old-fashioned dining hall with custom-made wallpaper. I waved goodbye to Arcadio Hardstone, who was very stressed near the house. He muttered something about getting back in time to the pool to stop his lovely friend, armadillo Jack, from killing a local peacock. It was unusual to see Arcadio so worried, and I wondered why I still cared for him after his mad accusations.

I stepped inside the house. The dining hall was quiet and empty. Still, someone snored upstairs. I knew exactly where the wheeze came from. Carefully, like a tiger, I climbed up to the last floor, facing the door to the Death Tower, the last obstacle to my privacy. I grabbed the doorknob. Suddenly, Alex Raphael opened the door from inside with a cup of hot liquid in his hand.

"Ah, it is you… Surprised to see you, Alex. How did you get here? I need a good breakfast, a shower, and lots of rest," my weak voice alerted him.

"I have no idea. I remember climbing out of Hamilton's car, but before and after that — only dim flashes." He paused. "We don't have a shower, but please, come in."

Alex Raphael welcomed me into the citadel of poverty and disaster. In the middle of the room slept Captain Happy, naked, on a smudged, wet, old mattress. The kettle was boiling on the floor in the far corner, spreading the aroma of oblivion and loss all around.

"Awful setting. What's next for you? Are you planning to find and locate your tourist group or maybe write a new book?" I joked.

"I'm going to work as a personal assistant for King

Hamilton. She is planning to publish a historical memoir about her deceased father. Don't worry, Mr. Harmless, I'm moving out to the American West Palace this afternoon."

"What is the American West Palace?" I asked with envy.

"Where kings live, of course."

We went out to the narrow two-square-meter balcony and sat side by side, breathing deeply, hating each other.

"Hamilton asked me to replace, at least for a couple of weeks, the priest of their Non-Binary Church. She begged me last night, hm, in her private rooms...," Alex Raphael paused. "I couldn't say 'no' after the second rough round. She knows how to make us, men, agree."

I made a slight shrug.

He continued, "I was able to save your photo, though. And the book."

Alex stood up, pulled out a crumpled picture from his shorts pocket, and placed it on my lap. From the photo smiled the one and only Margaret Thatcher. I hugged the shabby piece of paper, chaotically reciting the prayers I heard in my childhood, but the dream about peace was disturbed by the rattle on the door. Alex opened, inviting inside the lady of remarkable elegance, our host Ms. Sedative.

Her magical charm was supported by three other angels: Dinkie Dow, Blanca Speed, Spider Blue, who, without hesitation, jumped into the bed of the already awake Captain Happy.

"You are too perfect," I whispered, astonished by Ms. Sedative's brilliance.

"It's mother nature's gift," she replied. "And a skill mixed with money. More of skill and money, I'd say."

I didn't care. We stood and chatted for a couple of minutes. I complimented her on her beautiful mansion. She answered that her smoking area is even neater, fully renovated with a high-powered telescope, an intoxicating sauna, a magic whiskey brewery, and a self-discovery bed court.

"A telescope? What for?" I asked, surprised.

"To relax after a hard day of saving this kingdom from madness."

I nodded and glanced at Alex Raphael, hoping to receive some help, but he was busy entertaining our new arrivals: Holly Terror and Candy de Beast. The two young women brought with them a strange kind of fungus, full of the most lethal microbes, which, as they gladly explained, had been regularly used for a political purpose along the southeast coast of Screw Quarter. It was killing one-and-a-half million people every year in the other countries, too.

"Holly shit," I mumbled.

After an unintentional dance with Ms. Sedative, I started to see little red dots everywhere. I could touch tiny particles of dust. I could see beyond Neptune, seven billion miles away, beyond the Kuiper Belt, where my true love, Sobekneferu, resided. I felt trapped in the net of gross absurdist comedy, shifting my shapes, shouting about the desire to become a fossil, then seeing the astronauts passing above, waving and smiling. By the end of the evening, I had transformed into a Zombie of the Death Tower, incapable of conscious movements and designed to grow in one place only. Though, extremely slowly…

Within sixty-eight minutes of communication with Holly and Candy, I improved my tantric techniques and started to believe that my sexual abilities might be immortal.

The next three newcomers: Tootsie Heavens, Peth Backwards, and Drowsy High convinced me that I could last underwater for a few million seconds, suggesting an experiment, during which they'd sit on top of my lungs filled with a homemade soup from coyotillo berries that usually cause paralysis.

Like fleeting smoke, the room vanished. I couldn't predict anymore what was going to happen next. An ear-splitting scream woke me up, notifying me of the arrival of another of Ms. Sedative's servants.

"My name is Cecil Rippers. What a comfortable-looking place. I'm going to change that," she said.

Her words left me speechless. Ms. Rippers smiled with an expression of satisfaction and declared her latest discovery that dinosaurs aren't dead. I believed her.

It's safe to say that I was ready for a Dope yacht party.

a haircut selection

. . .

I WOKE up feeling that everything that happened in the Death Tower had been only a dream. Images of the visitors swept back and forth in my mind—their seductive voices, their sugary smell, their delightful touch—and slightly opened the window into strange reality, or the truth behind the insane asylum called Screw Quarter, filled with one hundred flirtatious patients who suffered from profound ego, mania, paranoia, and hallucination.

I was still slumbering when Ms. Sedative delivered my feverish body to the steps of the intimate saloon of Mrs. WickedBreaker. The owner reminded me of a *Big Momma's House* movie I watched when I was seven years old, indeed without any understanding of the situation in the film but nevertheless laughing with each appearance of the Big Momma actor on the screen.

Mrs. WickedBreaker took one look at me and said, "This isn't an ordinary fever. Place him in the Piranha room. Or wait… maybe he'd feel better in the Rebel corner."

Eight strong hands dragged me into the large room with a thick iron door. The entire moving procedure was carried out so light-heartedly that my whole body shook like a leaf.

"What women have you been with to get like this, poor child?" Mrs. WickedBreaker asked, slowly pulling blue latex gloves on her hands. The gloves were so long that they covered not only her arms and shoulders but also her neck.

"Women? I haven't been with any… it just happened," I lied.

"Squeaky clean guest? Here, in the Screw Quarter? I see, then most likely it is LKED," she said and checked a big oven with a brass pan upon it. Under a lock bubbled a hot liquid scented with paraffin. The idea of being cooked alive in this godforsaken town, without holding Sobekneferu in my arms, with no offspring, really bothered me.

Mrs. WickedBreaker turned out to be a very chatty woman who undoubtedly enjoyed the process of cutting and styling. While stirring the burning contents inside a pan, she told me that Screw Quarter was constructed as a place of pleasure, and Warrior Farm was constructed as their service providers.

"There's a balance, as you see. Or at least, there always have been until that nutty day when Alphonso Beard, the man—let me mention—with acute LKED illness, declared our state a dictatorship," she explained.

"But the farm has the right, in principle, to refuse to provide any service... It's a free land, isn't it?" I whispered.

"Depends to what extent... We have our values and laws, of course. If they refuse to provide whatever Hamilton Clan asks, then we can mark them as rebels. Father Dionysius was a rebellious man once." The woman took out a sharp razor and sighed. Her breasts, hiding behind a blue linen tee, swayed from emotional stress. "Until the day he became a non-binary member of our small and perfect society."

I recalled the expression of great horror in the priest's eyes from the moment he arrived at the raft till the last seconds of his life. Poor Father! I politely coughed, supporting the wave of memories in the air of the chamber and watching the dangerous moves of the gloves above my legs.

"What surprised me here, in Screw Quarter, was the ecclesiastic, erotic phenomenon of such welcoming culture—despite the limitations and borders of the kingdom—especially the force of it, a sense of modernity and sexual appetite in approaching male visitors," I said. I didn't dare ask the formidable lady of the intimate saloon about her personal experiences, but it seemed she was intrigued by my statement.

She replied, "Our new King Hamilton is too kind. Her father would throw all men in the pit behind the walls, where those needy creatures slowly but surely became the food of our poisonous insects."

The sinister development in our conversation

(stripped naked on a straight bench, with my hands chained behind my back) silenced me for a while.

"So, what will it be? Here is a catalog." The hostess dropped the enormous book on my belly and continued. "I'd advise to cut it all off. Under the root, so to speak…"

"Just because you are enjoying doing what you do doesn't mean it is the right thing to do!" I shuddered.

"Try not to complicate your life, doctor. Life is very, very simple and easy to understand."

"Then I want the simplest haircut you can offer!" I yelled. The chains began to chant the melody of Gashadokuro—a giant skeleton made of the bones of people who have died from injustice—notifying me of my future grim fate.

"When it's too simple, I lose any interest…," Mrs. WickedBreaker announced, offended by my proposal.

"Okay, let's start with something *more natural*: a boiling potato instead of potato salad?" I said.

The woman glanced at me, worried and full of tension.

"I'm not some kind of illusionist. Shut up and let me focus on my job, Dr. Harmless!"

She sealed my mouth with tape and tightened the chains. I fell into oblivion.

The touch of her fast hands and a generous injection of bourbon brought my senses back to reality. I looked down, squinting my eyes, trying to see the haircut under a transparent cloth, but all I could feel was the strange swelling in my crotch; everything around my phallus got bigger, as big as armadillo's head.

"This is one hell of a haircut!" I yelped.

"Anything you lose comes round in another form," Mrs. WickedBreaker patted me on the shoulder and quickly stepped out of the room. I assumed she had left me to grieve, but when eight strong hands grabbed me again, I realized that my haircut-torture was only beginning.

a dope party

. . .

WHEN I POKED out from Mrs. WickedBreaker's intimate saloon, it was as bright as day. The moon shone. Then, a cool breeze began to blow, and soon enough, the clouds covered the sky. I tried to sit down on the bench under the tree (it was a healthy motion my tired body needed, knowing what was to come), but my swollen haircut prevented me from such brutal action. Utterly jaded, I caught a glimpse of light far away, near the river. I went for it, cautious and slow.

The one percent of Gunung Kinabalu (members of Royal family, business magnates, world-class shopaholics of idle generation) stood near the luxurious yacht: finely dressed, speaking loudly to each other—a supermarket of perfect bodies blinking with neon smiles.

"It's nice to know somebody is happy," I murmured, while I creeped out from my hideout and approached the end of the long queue.

The yacht was custom-built, with extraordinary interiors from the famous Delilah Perfidiosus, Mr. Flamingo Vegas's second ex-wife. It was a beautiful boat, with seven cabins on each side, a stable with horses, two submarines, and what seemed to be a theater stage, right in the middle.

Ms. Glorious slowly descended from the twisted silver staircase, ran up to me, and said, "Po' po' little doctor! Here you are… you don't need to wait, sweetheart. Follow me; I have to dress you up for tonight's performance. I'm surprised Mrs. WickedBreaked had finished so late with you. Did you enjoy your treatment? We call her the delicious Demon of Gunung Kinabalu Paradise. Do you agree?"

The crowd froze. All eyes turned to my humble silhouette and started examining my body from head to toe. I felt uncomfortable, still smelling of paraffin and a moldy mattress.

"Of course, she is a nectarous lady," I answered, but my voice trembled. "Well, I don't want to waste a minute. Show me the way!"

On the yacht, in a stable, between twelve wild horses, twenty-five giant Japanese hornets, and 302 dead fire ants, I got to change into a long purple gown and a yellow feather-hair wig. After that, Ms. Glorious took me upstairs, where the crowd had already gathered. They stood around a colossal gold bowl filled with black Beluga sturgeon huso-huso caviar (which swims in the pollution-free waters of the Caspian Sea). King Hamilton and her three muscular sisters sat inside, kicking the water, and drinking the $18,600 Diamond is Forever Martini, with a price tag on each glass.

• • •

I didn't have time to look around, but I felt the one-hundred eyes that permeated me. Resigned to my fate, I went straight to the bowl and prepared to paddle for my life. At that moment, Mrs. WickedBreaker, who previously tore apart my penis, rolled up her sleeves and, with her hands up in the air, started to sing in a language I had never heard before.

Captain Happy, Alex Raphael, and Arcadio appeared on the stage, too: they took their positions in the corners. I noticed that Alex was dressed as a priest and looked very relaxed: he held a glass of milk in one hand and half a watermelon in the other. Arcadio wore a t-shirt with the word "Judge" on it. His armadillo Jack sat on the chair next to him with a crown DJ Hard-Core on his head.

"All right, trot ahead, fellas! Let's make Bullet remember this life party!" Martha shouted from the crowd.

It was only half-past two in the morning when the show started. Making rapid erotic rounds around the stage, I remarked that the sheriff tried to avoid me, but at the end of Dope festivity, crawling on the floor of the empty basin, I finally found her between the legs of three Hamilton sisters.

"Oh, hey... How's it going?" I asked.

"Last night, I had a dream about you and me in the pool, and I didn't like it one bit," she replied.

"It wasn't a dream."

"For real? I hate you, people!" she groaned.

"I'm not *people*! I'm Bullet, a man, an archeologist, a voodoo doctor, and... I fixed the haircut." Her words offended me. And it made me think about something I already knew—*run, it will get only worse, no better...*

Ms. Glorious, surprised by my strength and performance on the stage, hugged me and pulled me aside.

"Tonight, old friend, it's all about you and for you! Are you happy?" she whispered, patting my hair on the chest and making a duck face with her sweaty lips. When I refused to kiss her, she gulped more martini and continued, "Do you need to be back in Death Tower by any particular time?"

"No. Why?"

"Meet me at 7:00 a.m. near the American West Palace, in the garden."

"Bit late for... where is it? I have never been there. I can ask Alex; he moved in the palace last night."

"I know Alex very well," Ms. Glorious rolled her eyes dreamily. "King Hamilton is going to Beluga Clan with Arcadio this morning, so she left me in charge of her *palazzo*. It'd be crazy not to use it, right?"

"What about my trip to Warrior Farm?"

"Don't worry, Dr. Harmless. Our sheriff will take you there after lunch. She is the ex-wife of Alphonso Beard, the Body of Warrior Farm. She knows how to handle the man," Ms. Glorious winked.

"Okay. What about Captain Happy and Alex Raphael?"

There was a pause. The woman looked visibly upset.

"What about them?"

"I thought maybe you'd like to have a large company?"

"Let them stay where they are. Let them suffer!" she whinnied like a mad horse.

After our agreement, the red-haired beauty hid me inside of the damp room at the back of the yacht, where I met the first rays of sunlight. An odd panic, uncommon for a middle-aged man, passed through me, like lightning. I knew that Warrior Farm was full of women, too, but deep in my heart, I was hoping that they were busier and less hungry for *amour games* than in Screw Quarter. Because to be honest, after a Dope Party, I had lost interest in most things, including women.

american west palace

. . .

MS. GLORIOUS ESCORTED me to the narrow tunnel with a massive granite door. After three short knocks, we entered the so-called West Valley—the modern T-shaped central hall with an ugly row of chairs on both sides of the mainline. A team of highly qualified professionals approached us with forced smiles and greetings, guiding us to the learning chairs.

We sat quietly, with our throats strapped to the back, enjoying the roofless room's view. To overcome the fear of being rewired (or replicated somehow), I held my hand on Ms. Glorious' knee during the introductory process.

"It is perfectly placed," she murmured.

I lifted it promptly and explained, "It got there by accident."

"What high precision!"

Indeed, I was a man of accuracy and integrity. I flushed and directed my hand exactly to the north, aiming to connect to her perfectly designed G-system.

After a couple of minutes, we received the instructions. With a list of 111 rules in hand and the promise to repeat everything twice, we left to the opening at the end of the hall. The gates unlocked, and we stepped inside the beautiful magical land. It was like something from Aladdin's tales.

Perhaps an outsider, who had never been in such a mysterious place, could experience a feeling of mental excitement (or even oppression)— mostly from the sparks of power and sexual desire vibrating in every particle of the air, or from happy female faces, carelessly strolling on the road—but I was familiar with perplexing and enigmatic environments through my previous job.

I pulled up my uncomfortable shorts and joked, "O Hamilton, the King of the West, this palace is your true greatness! O semi-divine beings of unknown stars, how grateful I am that you came to me."

"Lovely words, doctor! Such a spiritual place, true… I'm getting goosebumps each time I'm entering it."

To say Ms. Glorious was in ecstasy from my sharp joke is to say nothing at all.

On the path to the king's chamber, which we went back and forth twice (following the rules established by local law), Ms. Glorious shared the latest news with me. I pretended to listen while my attention was captured by all that was going on: a bank made of crystal, an enormous music hall, gambling club, dating house, fight theater, moon-praying park, the tavern of joy and suffering, and half-naked women bathing in the colorful fountain filled with champagne and olives. An uninhabited island was being built nearby a commercial space line to Mars and Pluto. The Great Hamilton Pyramid, fresh and shining, occupied the eastern corridor of the palace. Each stone told the story of immense privilege, security, and perfection.

Everything was available in this place: sex, money, cars, drugs, luxury. Debauchery and greed were not an infection; this space was saturated with it. Or maybe it became a national need of the American West? I couldn't believe that the fulfillment of 111 rules and the power of the king could create order in this kingdom. It should be something else... something I couldn't grasp yet.

At some point, I returned my attention to Ms. Glorious, who was sharing a story about King Hamilton. As it turned out, the king kept more than 600 deer in her West Valleys. Every day, she'd bathe in a jade pool full of blood from these deer; then she'd powder her body with jasmine-scented anti-aging creams and continued her daily routines by playing sexual games with her devoted maidens or visitors (at random). Ms. Glorious thought it was an amusing, generous, and healthy activity.

As soon as she paused, I said, "It is such a boost for every visitor of Hamilton's Kingdom!"

"Yes, our West Palace is proof that miracles do happen." The woman smiled, luring me into the shadows. As you understand, *the miracle happened much sooner than I expected.*

Ms. Glorious peeled the layers of her clothing off. It

wasn't much—only her lotus triangle bra and floral mini strings in a beautiful combination of mesh and lace. I knew what to do: I was ready. I talked to her skin, to the thirst beneath it, to her hungry blood. After a short conversation, our blood raced together, and as you have probably guessed, we repeated it twice.

As we lay side-by-side, the all-powerful host of the Ark talked tenderly in whispers: "Hysteria is consuming our palace. Please, save it, Dr. Harmless! All hope is on you! There has been an epidemic of suicides in the kingdom in the last month, a wave of dark anger engulfing our throne. We understand that we are sending you into the mouth of the dragon. Warrior Farm is a fiend, where destruction is considered a good taste and where insubordination and murder are the signs of civilization. Every minute we live under the pressure of a fateful and terrible day called 'Awakening.'"

I mumbled (tortured by sleepless nights, longing for my Sobekneferu, drowning with wine, sex, and new crazy experiences): "I wouldn't mind staying here... Let's say taking a nap for half a century. Who knows, it might all work out by itself."

Without moving or smiling, Ms. Glorious looked at me, then knocking her tiny fists on the golden sand of the floor, exclaimed, "We can't allow any plebeians to decide how to rule our land! Screw Quarter's progressive ideas and the treasures of this country are already in the trash, Mister Bullet! Don't you see it?" she paused. "You are our avalanche, a brave snowball falling from the mountains, a cyclopean beast of science, the keeper of medical voodoo secrets, the fire in our patriotic hearts... We believe you can heal them from their madness!"

Her patriotism—kind and intense, the force of all good in the world—guided me directly to her smooth, silky skin. Ms. Glorious met my nervous strokes with sighs of satisfaction. I could feel the fierce shaking of her body under my rhythmical thrusts.

After that, we repeated everything twice, again.

some peculiar ways of love

. . .

'LOVE IS THE BEST MEDICINE.' *Who would disagree with this famous statement? Nothing changes our moods, effectively reduces stress, bolsters the ego, relieves backache, or lifts our self-esteem better than a good ol' love.*

After hours of indescribable pleasure, where each breath obeyed to my rhythm and tempo, I crawled to the couch near the window, frightened that I'd have to repeat it all over again. I knelt to check on my penis. Its crumpled blue skin aroused my suspicion—the end was near. I sighed and promised myself to save its precious life. At that moment, on the floor, I found a piece of stained paper—a photo of Margaret Thatcher. I smoothed the surface, lifted it closer to my eyes, and whispered, "Wherever life takes me, I know you'll follow me! The keeper of my secrets and sexual adventures, the old elite of rare stimulation!"

I was ready to confess all my sins of the day to Margaret's picture when the door swung open, and my ex-wife entered the room as some kind of farcical empress. Either from anger or envy, but the first thing she did (when she noticed that I was sitting on the floor with a photo of Margaret) was the jump of an angry leopard: she snatched a precious friend from my weakened hands, then violently tore the adorable image into tiny pieces—twice.

I couldn't move, perhaps from the inevitable pursuit of my ex-wife or from the dark figure of Alex Raphael, who stood behind her. He carried a dead peacock on his shoulder. I groaned, thinking, *what is an angel like me doing in this paradise of sinners?*

I stood up to greet my enemies (with a war-like attitude) who had just burst in, but only a bubbling sob escaped my lips. Or maybe it was a final goodbye: 1) to Margaret—the secret *aid* of my lonely nights in Rsa; 2) to my bus trips—the chanting movements of female hips during the morning ride to the museum; 3) to my sad but peaceful past—the dreams about the double door vaginas, slender waists, and larger breasts.

Suddenly, the room became as chilly as if it had been moved into February's open air. Martha settled down on the bedside table, and Alex laid the unconscious peacock on the bed next to the sleeping Ms. Glorious, who still didn't move.

"Dead?" I asked.

"Not yet. Sobekneferu is a regular visitor. She should be used to the speed of life in the American West."

"Sobe?" I coughed in shock, "K…Nefe…Ru?"

"It is one word, actually. Quite astonishing creature! I won her in poker," Alex Raphael grinned.

Martha looked at me sarcastically; she knew my latest obsession with Sobekneferu, the secret love of my life.

"Here she is, your lovffffe! Delivered to the door," Martha laughed and whistled at the end. That whistle woke up Ms. Glorious from a dreamless nap. Her face was as red as her hair. She looked worn out. Despite that, she threw herself over Alex's body and started to sniff all over his chest like a hunting dog. Alex found himself totally helpless, looking at her goddess-carved shape of white jade with two ripe red cherries. He instinctively began to respond... I managed to pull out a half-dead bird from under the voluptuous movements of two lovers.

I ran out of Hamilton's chambers and rushed to the stairs. Sensing a chase behind my back, I turned sharply. Sobekneferu's feathers left red streaks on Martha's wrathful face.

I shouted desperately, "For Lovffffffe!" and repeated the turn twice.

Without hesitation, I continued my wild escape from the West's madness down the stairs to the gates of freedom, but an iron grip paused my motion.

"Are you trying to steal the symbol of our strength and beauty? She is Screw Quarter's favorite party animal!" the sheriff asked.

With a submissive expression on my face, I explained, "The opposite! I am trying to revive your symbol from the Land of Dead using the latest medical technologies."

The sheriff suspiciously glanced at Martha's bleeding cheeks and said, "Ms. Downhill Tasty asked about you, Martha. She needs help in the kitchen. Or do you want to follow Dr. Harmless to Warrior Farm?"

"I just wanted to save your symbol from the mouth of this hungry, dirty lion. Don't be fooled by his innocent words!" Martha played victim.

Seeing the spark of a question in the sheriff's eyes, I snapped. "This is a lie! I love Sobekneferu regardless of its shape in the real world."

The sheriff grabbed me by the shorts, took my hands from the still deranged bird, and threw me into the room under the stairs.

"Get some sleep, doctor. You've done enough here!"

I accepted my destiny, pleased with the gentleness in the sheriff's voice. Then, I adjusted my eyes to the gloom of the room, observing the space around me. Between a grey kimono in thin silk and a blinking phone, Armadillo Jack snored. He was attached to the wall by a chain and seemed profoundly satisfied by the world around him. I stroked Armadillo's hair, listening to my neurotic racquet-beating heart, and mumbled, "Sweet dreams, madame Jack… you can't even imagine how happy I am to see you. You are the most beautiful beast with a mobile phone!"

Perhaps you won't believe me, but I felt how the strange strong force started to grow inside of me—rejuvenating, healing, beautiful as a ray of the sun playing on the tail of a peacock. *I was truly an avalanche, a brave snowball falling from the mountains, a cyclopean beast of science, the Master of Medical voodoo…* I was the King of the world, the one that was much bigger than the American West, Screw Quarter, or Gunung Kinabalu. I grabbed the phone and dialed my mother.

the gossips

. . .

"THAT'S another thing I don't understand," my mother interrupted my incoherent words' livestream, "Why you, of all people in Rsa, should save those poor sick souls in that desolate wild land? You aren't a doctor!"

For a second, I stopped my confused revelation and asked myself, *Really, how did it happen? Why am I here? What was the reason in the first place?* To my shame, I realized, the answer was quite simple— perpetual horniness. After the divorce, my body and mind had been constantly plagued by a profound thirst for romance, by which I mean fucking a real woman instead of jerking off to images of explicit porn or the tight bathroom conversation with Thatcher's smile.

"I used to ask myself that all the time, Mom… I guess I just got caught up in the middle of it all. So, to speak, unfortunate circumstances… or maybe the God of Luck, Shai, brought his misfortune down on me? Because as it is written in the divine instructions of

Amenemope, 'Do not set your heart upon seeking riches, for there is no one who can ignore Shai; do not set your thought on lustful matters, for every man, there is his appointed time,'" I cited.

Armadillo Jack looked curiously at my blushing face, awakened by the heat of the conversation in the dwarfish room of his personal restoration.

"Please, don't be so melodramatic!" my mother hissed over the phone.

I gave a weak smile towards the damp wall and continued, "I'm not a brave man, Mom."

"I'm glad we agree on some things," she replied with satisfaction.

"And I'm not a saint either… Don't worry, I'll make our family proud!"

"It's better this way," she concluded before delivering the latest gossip from Rsa.

My parents lived half an hour from my town in a small village called *The Big Pump*. My mother was the gossip queen of the community thanks to her unique position—she was the book club chairman and a local fortune-teller. The book club was named 'Anime Antiqua' and often charged members (who had not had time to read the whole book or could not answer my mother's carefully prepared questions) penalties.

Without asking me, she shared the information about her latest read, Ann Radcliffe's book, *The Mysteries of Udolpho*. She told me that during our short conversation, she noticed the similarities between me and Emily St. Aubert, who had been kept imprisoned by her rapacious guardian and his sadistic wife. After those words, I attempted to break my mother's sick ideas, making an effort to convince her that my arrival in Hamilton's Kingdom is not a Gothic battle in some gloomy medieval fortress, and most of all, I'm not an orphaned hero with melancholy fancies or pensive visions. Of course, my mother didn't agree with me because she saw *The Mysteries of Udolpho* as a landmark of psychological pre-Freudian exploration of the psyche.

"O Heavens! Am I a psychopath now?" I exclaimed, feeling that I was losing the verbal war. But as always, I had to accept that my mother was right, primarily, when she passed on the dangerous information from Mr. Vegas and Mr. Domination, which had been transmitted via the local channels for the past week. Apparently, my name was top of the most wanted list in Rsa.

"Can I get you anything, my boy?" asked my father's voice in the far distance.

"He can't hear you, Pilgrim," my mother replied to him.

"If you are unhappy about your penis, then it's fixable," my father continued. I heard the fight near the phone. It seemed that mother defended her position, and not only with words. Something heavy dropped on the floor, and she sighed, "It is so hard to be a mother."

Then, she extended our chat and overwhelmed me with various suggestions about medical books I should read. She even came up with a couple of dangerously mad plans to escape Gunung Kinabalu without a fight.

I sat and listened, but my heart was full of anguish —I understood, more clearly than ever, that life goes on.

Nothing changed in Rsa: a hard-boiled life joyfully passed from one to another, so-and-so would vanish or die, and nobody cared about it.

I didn't hear when sheriff entered the room. The rays of the sun behind her were like orange velveteen, and it gave a warm glow to her surprised face.

"What is that?" the sheriff hissed.

"What is *what*?"

I gave my voice as much innocence as I could. Then, I followed her angry gaze to my right hand where the screen of my unfinished call shone in blue and green, and my mother's voice shouted, "Take a picture of this barbarian, I want to see if she is real... She speaks like that witch, Martha."

I quickly ended the call. "Let us go," I demanded. "The humidity in this room is unhealthy for my jaded brain cells!"

The anxiety mixed with terror escalated in my voice. I could almost read the armadillo's eyes: "If you can't handle some tiny chick from the Screw Quarter, how the fuck are you going to handle 11,000 bitches at the farm?!"

I climbed up, pressing my back to the moist wall, but fell.

The sheriff smirked, looking down at my funny position: "Alphonso Beard is waiting for your arrival at the Warrior Farm. Let's go, Doc!"

I silently followed her out, crawling on all fours.

the forest lovers

. . .

I WOKE up on the grass in the woods, covered by a greasy napkin, a hundred bright yellow beetles with black markings, and sheriff's lifeless naked body. I lay on my back and tried to breathe steadily.

"What a mess! This is the result of your sexual ego, Bullet," I said aloud, looking at the moonlight.

It is not that I object to this kind of game, mind you, I like the fresh leaves, loose rocks, warm soil, deserted caves, and the sound of the water—it all turns me on. I can make love outside for hours if there's decent bug spray or a hot woman. But the idea of killing during sexual intercourse, especially the local sheriff on duty, made me fear for my sanity, freedom, and life. *Did I do it?*

I crawled out from under the sheriff's body that had become cold and heavy. Ironically, the beetles disapproved of my escape; they ejected some intensely acrid fluid on my feet, which immediately started to burn. I could feel the strength draining out of me and waves of persistent faint nausea flowing through me. Despite the pain, I stood up and looked around.

I recalled how we stopped near a beautiful waterfall surrounded by overgrown brambles.

"Here it is—our royal cemetery! There's no better spot in the world where you can let go of your worries, duties, and curious eyes," the sheriff explained.

I understood she was familiar with the area when she invited me inside of the hidden grotto down the path. There, she took off her purple kimono and began to sponge her breasts with the muddy, cold water. Anxious, I pulled down my trunks, presenting to her sight the latest cut from Mrs. WickedBreaker. The sheriff's excitement and the nod of her head made me tremble.

"Stop shaking!" she ordered.

"Sorry, my body vibrates by itself," I tried to control my twitching knees.

As I stood there, holding my penis in the ready position, I felt as if I had been struck in the back with a club. Then, the same firm hand splintered that club above my head. I made a surprised noise and fell to the ground.

"A greasy napkin?" I picked it up and sniffed it. It should be some kind of clue, I knew that, but I had a splitting headache, plus, I had to deal with the disposal of the sheriff's body. Unfortunately, I couldn't get back to the Screw Quarter and ask them for help because Hamilton's sisters would gladly lynch me. And just when I had given up all hope (as it always happens in novels and fairytales), I caught a strange white glimmer amongst the trees on the opposite side of the royal cemetery. At first, I thought it was a zombie, who'd like to eat the brains I don't have; then, I thought it was a mysterious horny ghost who'd dreamed of shaking my stupid body until I'd become invisible, too.

The humid blackness crept slowly over me. I stood breathless, waiting. After a couple of minutes, I heard a cranky voice behind my back. I wasn't able to decipher the message as it had been pronounced in the local language. I was ready to meet my opponent, but when I turned and saw the bulky, tall sack-body, covered in brown filth with a horn in his (or her) hands, weighing 180 pounds, I screamed and fled, leaving sheriff's dead body behind me.

"Are you alright?" a worried voice above my face brought me back to my senses.

"I don't know. I think I saw a long-haired snowman near the royal cemetery."

"Probably Ms. Sweet Hellfire? She is our dentist. Wild-life and wicked insects are her hobbies. She will be very helpful to you, Dr. Harmless, if I'm not wrong, hehe, you are working in the same field."

The man smiled and stretched out his hand to me. "My name is Ale de Sandwich. I am the first assistant of our Body, the Head of the Warrior Farm, our Apollon of Fierce Power, or simply, Mister Alphonso Beard. It's such a proud moment for us all to welcome you in our town." He paused. "Your castle, your seven housekeepers, and full English breakfast are ready and waiting. How was your trip? I've heard that the sheriff had planned to escort you to our gates."

. . .

I stretched my legs with the help of the caring Ale de Sandwich and replied, "We had a pleasant trip, but then rain suddenly splashed the road, and we hid in the cave… I fell asleep. It seems the sheriff left the grotto in the middle of the night, and I have not seen her since."

"Hm, she may have met Ms. Sweet Hellfire and told her to take care of you. That's my explanation!" the man laughed carelessly.

"I hope she didn't," I whispered.

"You don't happen to remember which of the grottos it was, do you? We have so many located on the different ages of our farm."

"No, I don't. How many are there?" I was annoyed by his presence but couldn't decline his honeyed hospitality.

"Hundreds, I believe. Only Ms. Sweet Hellfire knows. Ah, there she is…"

I glanced to my left. A dark spot, something with rough, grey, oily hair, moved towards me.

"Morning, Ale! Let me take care of our precious guest!" Ms. Hellfire said in English.

When the fully satisfied assistant left us, she stopped, took my panicked face in her hands, and declared, "If you don't marry me, I'm going to tell Alphonso Beard that you killed his ex-wife in the woods."

"But I didn't do it."

"Listen, it's either marriage or death. What's it going

to be, Dr. Harmless?" The monstrous yeti-woman grinned.

It took only 0.0000000003 seconds. I gazed one more time at her solid arms. '*What the hell,* and decided, *I'll take my chances.'*

I shouted, "Death!"

evolution of marriage

. . .

NOTHING IS MORE *terrifying than sudden and unpredictable change, especially the loss of freedom. That's why we are so frightened by marriage.*

Everything around me went black for a moment. The pores all over my body—disturbed, spongy, sieve-like—gave a strange, long, loud noise when Ms. Sweet Hellfire took out a six-foot rubber hose from her right sleeve and aimed at me. Pictures of instant torture danced inside of my head. I wondered, *shouldn't they first interrogate a suspect? Do they have a real jail? Will I ever see my mother again?* but instead, I asked my tormentor, "What have I done wrong?"

"Nothing. I just like it. And it's far more effective than simply killing you," Ms. Sweet Hellfire explained.

I listened in agony. Meanwhile, the Warrior Farm's monster continued, "You know, when it whacks against your skinny ass, at first, it bites into your flesh, and then it sticks out a bit… inch-by-inch. It is so lovely!"

To say my skin crawled and my blood oozed out after her short and serene confession is to say nothing at all. My lust has been my punishment; because the woman, Sobekneferu Queen, the one I wanted to find, has nourished a strange passion, which became my doom and my misery.

"Don't worry; I'm going to beat a bit of sense into you, Dr. Harmless, my soon-to-be husband!" Ms. Sweet Hellfire added.

Needless to say, after that shocking revelation, I surrendered to her powers. With extended arms, I welcomed her purgatory intentions with a scream of joy.

On the following day, I woke up in the cave. Instinct—or perhaps an alarming sense of self-preservation—made me leave the place in a rush, and I tripped and fell near the entrance. Only then did I notice that I wore green knitted trousers, a yellow t-shirt, and pink slip-on heel sandals. My heart pounded with fear. I had no recollection of changing clothes. In hopes of escaping the benefits of a morning romp, I hurried out, jogged down from the top of the mountain, where a cave was located, and looked over my shoulder in the direction of the place where I spent last night.

Of course, I tried to convince myself that Ms. Sweet Hellfire would forget about the marriage as soon as the next male guest arrived. But I was wrong... Two days later, I stood in the white chapel dressed like a king, reading words on a paper with poor enthusiasm.

"O Holy Saints! My dearest angel, Ms. Sweetest Hellfire, let me come in. I have lived in this glorious world alone for too long, and I had never experienced such amazing delights of Eros until you woke me up. Never, till this moment, did I know what true love is… Let me come in."

"My door is locked," flirted Ms. Sweet Hellfire under the soft and shadowy hint of the glowing screen. The screen was connected to the house of each citizen of this dreadful town.

"I have a key," I replied, hesitating with what I was supposed to do next: read the rest of the text, kneel, kiss the bride, or wait for approval from the blue screen.

"O blessed key! Please, liberate me! Us!" Ms. Sweet Hellfire shouted.

After that anguished howl, absolute terror deprived me of my body. I sunk, senseless, on the floor. My bride tried to tranquilize my spirits and elevate my 'key' somehow, but anxiety made me constantly shake or faint. Ms. Sweet Hellfire enjoyed that exhausting suspense.

The next few hours passed in agitated conversation between the bright screen and my 'newborn, complementary' wife. I was unaware of most of the drama that occurred around me, but I did a couple of stretches on the floor and watched how the sun's rays faded slowly behind the windows. The conversation ended, and the blue screen switched off. After that, tense melancholy took over the walls in the giant wedding room. Pulse, breathing, rustle—it was too quiet around me. I thought that Mrs. Sweet Hellfire had decided I was dead or passed out because of my inborn shyness and weak heart, but I left those hopes when I felt a firm grip on my shoulder.

"I believe it will be very long before I forget myself in sleep today," Mrs. Sweet Hellfire groaned. She took off her wedding dress, then her warm jacket under the dress, and began to roll up the sleeves of her furry lingerie. Then, she grabbed my body and threw it on the luxury king-size round bed.

Her eyes expressed the dark passion of rare sweetness (it was uncommon, especially for a dentist), with a slight symptom of madness.

That groan was so human, I thought but said nothing.

"Don't worry, darling Harmless. It will be a night worth remembering!"

A strong survival impulse, which I had inherited from my poor father, gave me the energy to raise my hand and look at our marriage certificate with a man's I'd never met signature—Alphonso Beard.

"No, please, no... Sobekneferu...," I whispered in a shaky voice. "One day, I'll find you, I promise, even if I have to get back from the land of dead."

From the far corner of the room, the drums and the trumpet started to play the last dance wedding song. I made one more effort to hide between the pillows but was stopped by my wife's strong hands.

"It won't help," she grabbed a heavy bed and pulled it out of the chapel. We continued our journey to a remote location, far from the blue screen, the music, the moon, Alphonso Beard, or any civilization. And there, in the darkness, I said aloud for the last time, "Sobekneferu…," enjoying my own echo.

the face of tyranny

. . .

THE WARRIOR FARM was the first place in the Gunung Kinabalu Kingdom that had all the usual features any town in the world has: a pond with a big park, a market, a bank, a big circus with sexy acrobats, a police force, a strong army, an excellent high-tech hospital, landline phones, and post office. It looked civilized and reminded me of my hometown, Rsa.

My private castle with seven housekeepers (who I hadn't met yet) was located in the Prudent Village—the Warrior Farm's headquarters. I decided to take a walk there because, luckily enough, Ms. Sweet Hellfire had a new appointment with Alphonso Beard's thirty-fourth wife (she got a painful toothache last night). Of course, my wife wasn't happy about leaving me alone. She looked as if she wanted to scratch my eyes out when I gladly explained to her about my decision to visit my estate this morning, and perhaps to spend the night in separate bedrooms.

She picked up her dentistry implements—razor-sharp and extremely hard—and came closer to me. I dreaded her next move, and I was right to fear: my wife began to shed her fur. Under her skin, just as I expected, hid the ugliest creature with colorless eyes, rotten teeth, and greenish skin.

I pursed my lips in a soundless whistle, "Can you slow it down a bit, wifey? I don't know if I'm ready for this kind of change..."

I wanted to walk away, but Mrs. Sweet Hellfire was faster: she grabbed my legs, hung me upside down, and injected my neck with some hydrazaline-pentazalicine-domino-porfinatus drug. My body went limp.

I woke up in my castle.

"How's your appetite?" asked the sweetest voice above my head. "I'm Alphonso Beard's second assistant, and my name is Ms. Break de Roof."

I opened my eyes wider, feeling how the sea of hot flames ran through my veins. The woman who spoke to me was blonde, young, and fresh, with smooth olive skin and provocative grey eyes.

"Let's *break* everything we can," I said.

She gave a wild, choked scream, then threw herself on my chair, knocked me down on my back, and started to sniff my yellow knitted pants, nibbling and blowing wildly, left and right. After that odd operation, she abruptly stood up, walked to my head, then turned around and lifted her leg to climb over me. Slowly, she lowered herself down while stroking her breasts down my face. Only then did she finally free my iron-hard *warrior* from its prison. I smiled, expecting to see the rest of such a welcoming gesture. To my surprise, Ms. Break de Roof glanced down at my wild forest, chuckled, and stopped her sliding body-to-body process. She quickly changed her position and said, "Well, we can't stay in bed screwing all the time, Dr. Harmless. You have your professional duties; our president would like to meet you to discuss LKED disease. Ah, and don't forget your lovely wife."

"I'd rather kill myself than spend one more night with her," I confessed.

"Give her a chance. Ms. Sweet Hellfire *fasted* for too long."

"Because nobody wanted her?" I joked.

"Not necessarily… Her husband died a month ago, and we are still in the stage of mourning."

"No wonder he died. Do you know the reason?" I replied.

"I heard some rumors… According to the first assistant, her husband was poisoned, but we never investigated it properly," she sighed. "I suppose you'd like to know the truth… I've heard you are a detective."

I nodded.

She continued, "But you still have to prove to our Board that you didn't kill the sheriff. Not that I care much, but she was one of us once. I think the brain of our community, the Head of the Warrior Farm, our Apollon of Fierce Power, or simply Alphonso Beard was in love with her… strongly. She was his favorite ex-wife and a member of Hamilton's inner circle. As you have probably guessed, she delivered the information we needed: mostly about the deals between Beluga Clan and The Screw Quarter. When we lost our best spy, we had to find and train a new one, which takes time. I hope you get that? And time is something we don't have, Dr. Harmless. Our people are dying."

I didn't care much about the town or the people. I wanted her breasts on my face, moving up and down like they were a few minutes ago.

"My dearest, Ms. Break de Roof, something in those knitted pants is dying from thirst, too," I whispered, shaking from lust. I hoped that in her last words had been hidden some cryptic meaning about our 'soon-to-happen' erotic session.

"What if you are contagious? Did you figure out a cure for LKED?" she asked doubtfully.

"How so? I didn't encounter any sick citizens yet. Can you give me some idea of the nature of LKED?" I frowned.

"We have confidence that people who are sick—at least, most of them—are going through the shedding process," the second assistant sadly explained.

I pictured my wife this morning, the changes she went through in her look, and I felt sorry for myself. Then, just as I was standing in front of a giant stone table, I noticed a persistent, rending, sweet smell. I opened the pan wrapped in bamboo leaves: there lay seven raw eyeballs in a sauce of unknown origin. The rays of the sun did a perfect job on that dish; wicked worms of different kinds savored the juices, changing the color of the bloody eyes to green. I have to admit, it wasn't my definition of tasty and healthy.

While I was busy with my two-week-old breakfast, Ms. Break de Roof mysteriously disappeared. I was disappointed, but the hunger in my belly called for a real meal. I rang the bell. Seven beautiful, perfectly dressed housekeepers entered the dining room. Each of them had a tail—a Bluetooth or wi-fi-connected animatronic tail that only the real owner could control. As I understood, the tail allowed the wearer to express emotions without any conversation.

"Hello, ladies! I called you to change my morning meal. I can't eat those raw eyeballs; I am a vegan. I'd prefer something simple, like eggs with bacon," I ordered.

All seven tails made the erect tremble movement.

"It's not what in the food, it's what's been done to the food that matters," the mechanical male voice from the wall answered.

Astonished, I turned to the glowing screen. I knew, somewhere inside there's a watcher with a remote control. By the tone of his voice, I could tell that the person enjoyed the game. I was a delicious little toy to him. I shivered and leaned against the wall.

"Well, I'm happy to see you are willing to help me, ladies. Good work, you all. You can leave now... please?" Unconsciously, I clasped my hands together and kneeled in a praying position.

They didn't listen. With big smiles on their faces and the Happy Wag dance of their tails, they surrounded me in a circle and cornered me in the chair. Fourteen hands quickly wrapped my body in some sticky curtain

—tightly, around, and around—and fed me the two-week-old breakfast.

"Everything is okay?" the cheerful head of Ale de Sandwich popped out from the door.

"Everything is great, The First Assistant!" the sharp voice from the blue screen announced. The seven housekeepers wagged their tails with pride and joy. *The Warrior Farm town reminded me of the words from the book of Jean Racine: "The face of tyranny is always mild at first..."*

alphonso beard or how to become a leader

. . .

SOMEONE SHOOK MY HAND, calmly and methodically, as if testing my reaction to the surrounding reality, which was so indescribably sad in the previous days that, finally, I was ready to surrender and accept the tragic fate that foreshadowed my "miserable" future in the Warrior Farm. I grabbed the new guest's arm with my trembling hands. When my eyes leveled on the face of a powerful intruder in my dining room, a scream froze on my lips. His head was fully covered by an animated panda mask. A mask that would be authentic were it not for the odd glasses and a small red funny hat on the top of the panda's head. The man laughed, pushing my sticky hands away from his spotless suit.

A sound of dread filled the space around us. The panda-man said, "For Apollon's sake, shut the fuck up, will you? My name is Alphonso Beard; I've been waiting to meet you, Mr. Harmless. I've wanted to thank you for your brave decision to access the sick in our closed community of brave warriors. We, the people of Gunung Kinabalu, can't tell you how much that means to us." He paused, then went to the opposite wall and pressed two invisible buttons. The sides of the wall moved apart, and to my surprise, he entered the most gorgeous library in the world. The room was about 378 feet long and 411 feet wide, with barrel-vaulted ceilings built in the shape of a flower. The floor was covered in multi-colored tiles.

"I have something for you," the mask continued, pulling out an oddly shaped book from the endless shelves. "I wrote that in the first month of my arrival to the Warrior Farm. Since then, I have never stopped writing... Of course, I had some necessary breaks with all the excitement of never-ending love affairs and then the LKED issues, but this town would never survive without me. I am the opposite of chaos!"

The library room stored 18,000 volumes of Alphonso Beard's books on every topic of life, such as science, medicine, philosophy, sex, military, and law. I looked at the titles on the covers: *How to Act Like a King, How to Play on People's Need to Believe if you Want to Create a Cult-like Following, How to Fool your Wife, Colleague, Companion, or Enemy.*

"Are they all how-to books?" I asked, intrigued by the titles.

"Yes. Is it that obvious?" Alphonso laughed. It seemed the man behind the mask was thrilled by my reaction.

"How to Enjoy Life on Warrior Farm: Guide for Dr. Harmless. Chapter 1: Be the only one who can do what

you do. The more people want you, the freer you are. Make people depend on you for their health, happiness, or prosperity… and you have nothing to fear," I read aloud.

"This booklet is my welcome gift to you," the ruler of the town added. "Because believe it or not, you are really one of the nicest doctors I've ever met. And we've had a few in the past half-year."

"What happened to the previous doctors?" I asked.

"They died."

"What if I die, too?"

"Well… I'll miss you. We all will."

Alphonso Beard was eager to share his achievements with me: he was the one who loved to brag, play, and kill. He invited me to visit one of his castles. I thanked him for the rare opportunity and announced my desire to leave immediately: I was feeling suffocated in my new house.

Palace #77 looked quite simple on the outside—a white cubic base topped with a black cylinder. We walked in, took the stairs to the cylindrical part that was lined with thousands of bookshelves. We went up to the top, to the open bar, and sat on the ugly green chairs facing the sunset. Alphonso Beard poured me a drink.

"How is your thirty-fourth wife feeling? I heard she had some trouble with her teeth last night."

"She is fine, Doc. Our wonderful Mrs. Sweet Hellfire reinstalled all her teeth. I might visit her tonight; all that thinking about flesh and new mouth usually makes me really horny."

I coughed, "I wonder how a busy man like you can handle so many wives? For example, how do you remember all their names?"

"There's a guide for that in the library," the mask replied. "It is called *Always Say Less than Necessary*. By the way, my thirty-fourth wife is from Bolivia, Mrs. Hydra UnstoppableTide. She arrived at the Warrior Farm to become a simple baker... Ah, the most extraordinary baker, I must admit, but I made her my wife and the Judge of the Board Committee. You'll meet her soon enough, Dr. Harmless," Alphonso said as he placed his empty glass on the napkin with the infinity circle.

An eerie thought pierced through me. I had seen that sign of two rings before, in the cave where the cold body of the sheriff had been left to rot. We looked at each other, a flicker of tension between us.

"You need to rest, Doc. Tomorrow, at 6:00 a.m., we'll meet again at the Board meeting, where you'll have to prove your innocence in the matter of the sheriff's murder."

"It will be easy," I said with triumphant confidence.

"No doubt, we know it was Mrs. Sweet Hellfire."

"What is the sentence for the murder in your country?"

"The punishment is very mild: a) the slave market in the Back-Block Province; it's located on the border with the Beluga Clan. Or b) a hundred thousand blows on the Peace Square in the middle of our town. Let me assure you, either way, you'll be fully satisfied, Dr. Harmless. You can always marry my second assistant; I've heard you were truly impressed when you met her this morning."

I didn't say anything. I needed time to think.

inside of the box

. . .

I SAT IN THE BEDROOM, surrounded by the piles of how-to books, trying to make sense of Alphonso Beard's sophisticated writing. Unfortunately, even my university degree couldn't help me to understand his tips. I fell asleep, exhausted from reading, with my eyes swollen from the constant tension. I heard the arrival of Mrs. Sweet Hellfire, who went upstairs and started to bang impatiently on my bedroom door, craving sexual services. I put some earplugs in and hid my head under the pillow.

At 4:00 a.m., I plucked up the courage and went to the bathroom at the end of the hall. Because I could no longer share my worries with Margaret Thatcher's photo, I was forced to talk to my own reflection in the mirror. That man inside of the mirror on the wall wasn't me, or maybe he was me, partly, but the one I've tried to keep locked away for years. He was dressed in crumpled pajamas and looked dissatisfied and weak. I hated him.

"I'll rejoice every second you are with me, Bullet, and that will be most of the time, day and night. Our life is so short," said a voice behind my back.

"We've got different visions on life and marriage, Mrs. Sweet Hellfire. Sometimes I need to be alone, and probably more often than you'd be expecting," I sighed and prepared for the worst.

My wife came closer, placed a silver feather under my chin and started to move it down to my belly, intent on erecting my unwilling-to-work antenna. I glanced down at her green mouth, full of poisonous saliva, and I knew that if I'd died tonight, then the words on my grave would read: *He couldn't manage it.*

I didn't die. At six sharp, I was standing at the Meeting Hall's door, waiting to be invited to the mysterious Board Meeting. The door opened, and two guards unceremoniously dragged me inside. The walls in the hall were made of limestone, with six dramatic arches springing from enormous masonry piers. The mosaic floor was made of strips of yellow and blue marble. Each side provided access to the roof above with the help of the spiral stairs.

One of the guards put an empty brown card box above my head, tied my hands behind my back, and pulled me towards the stairs. I shouted that I could walk by myself, but they held me fast. After the sixth floor, I lost count.

. . .

I woke up because my body—utterly exhausted from the nights with Mrs. Sweet Hellfire and constant food collisions with seven housekeepers—was pierced to the floor by unbearable pain. Something wet and heavy fell on the box; the guards laughed. One of them said it was Bubbly, the local bird with abnormally big droppings. After a minute or two he removed the dirty card box from my head. I looked around. We were standing on the roof of a building with the centrally located Information Desk. Behind the desk sat an old lady who asked the guards something in the local language.

Satisfied with the response, she pressed a red button and ordered them to strip me off and replace the dirty box with a clean one. The guards followed her orders with pleasure. I wanted to ask the lady in charge how long we had to wait and what exactly we were waiting for, but the guards started to talk, and their strange conversation stopped me from any inquiries.

"He's not too bad-looking, or at least, he wouldn't be if we'd put some clothes on him again."

"You don't understand a thing… This is the latest fashion outside of Gunung Kinabalu—brisk and spicy. Look, the horrifying face of snake-haired erection is aimed directly at you, Jellywobble," the man laughed.

"Don't be absurd, Medusa."

"Ah, I sometimes envy all those outside freedoms we guards don't have. Don't you, Jellywobble? Deep down, all we want is to be naked."

"Only as a metaphor."

"I'm telling you; change is in the air."

"Maybe, but the Board is a true challenge. I hope Dr. Harmless is flexible enough."

"I hope. I remember my night with a previous doctor. It was so opaque, so boring… I didn't understand it at all. You know how I adore all tips in the *How To Perform Infinite Sex* book, but he just didn't get it, that pure, uncluttered idea of shifting positions upside down."

"Some people are not prepared to face your reality, Medusa."

"Yeah… we are living in a scary time, Jellywobble."

"What we need is war because then the men from Beluga Clan would visit us more often and finish our daily suffering."

"The rumors go that they are all castrated; that's why they are fighting."

"What? Noooo! You just destroyed all my hopes, Mr. Medusa! I must visit a teahouse room immediately; I feel so broken," the old lady behind the Information Desk added.

A hatch in the floor opened at that moment, and a familiar voice ordered, "Drop the doc, we are ready!"

Two guards, Medusa and Jellywobble, pushed me down into the hatch. Someone lifted the box from my head. It was the fifth Mrs. Vegas—a gentle soul from Rsa, full of frantic tricks in the field of tantric love.

"Mrs. Delight, what are you doing here?" I asked, shocked.

"Shh… I'm here to help you. I'm Alphonso Beard's next wife. Our wedding is tomorrow," Mrs. Vegas whispered.

"How are you going to help me?"

"I'm on the Board. I'm going to save your miserable life, Mr. Harmless, but you must promise me something."

"Mm… what?"

"Just promise."

"Okay."

She put the box on my head again, leaving me shaking in the shadows of fear. I made a promise to help, but I was the one who needed it the most.

the board of eyes

. . .

I NEVER KNEW darkness could vibrate—through the waves of macabre curse dancing on its own—wrestling with the mindset of ordinary individuals like me while re-modeling my pessimistic reality. No doubt, a combination of increasing wealth, foreign stimulation, and political instability throughout the Warrior Farm allowed that darkness to flourish. I felt how the air sang and spun, making my heart 'tick' in a sad abnormal way.

The portraits of women—perhaps, Alphonso Beard's previous wives—hung on the walls above the long line of tombs and broken skulls. I noticed the play of the curious hues in the twilight of the stones as if they invited me to share my life force with them. So far, my extraordinary journey was a fabulous adventure in search of Sobekneferu. Still, the nostalgia of seeing my little town Rsa again, as well as having thought-provoking conversations with my boss, Mr. Killing, and most importantly, the traditional tea parties at my mother's house made me long for home.

Eventually, all good things must come to an end, I thought, while watching a dozen artificial flying eyes invade the room to shock me. I waved my hands left and right in a naïve attempt to pose as a real fighter. The most spectacular thing I had achieved was an erection.

The floor creaked beneath me: two unusual items suddenly appeared in the center. One of them was a silver chair encrusted with diamonds. Another was an elegant, freestanding golden bathtub, clean and shiny. I selected a small area between the bath and the demonic chair and secured my position in a highly visible location.

"Do you know that the previous doctor is buried right under your feet? Together with my thirteenth ex-wife, each of them mummified and in its own small coffin," asked Warrior Farm's ruler. The eyes, intrigued or angry, began to buzz and swirl around the spot where I stood, waiting for an answer.

"I didn't know, but thanks for sharing it with me. I guess this makes quite an impression on new visitors of the Meeting Hall," I replied.

"Let me remind you, we keep a detailed record of all our conversations in a digital format. Can we proceed, Judge?" asked Alphonse in a calm voice. Only then did I realize that I was not alone in the room: Mrs. Hydra was standing right behind me. She held something flashing in her hands—a shocking electric whip.

"Shoot!" Mrs. Hydra barked. She moved from one

corner to another, enjoying my trembling appearance. In my mind, I had convinced myself that I had already lived far longer than it might have been expected in this area of sick wilderness, and luck was not on my side. Not this time…

The procedure began. I don't know how many odd medical questions I answered before two women of an eerie beauty entered the room and filled the bathtub with warm red filth. They invited me to relax before the next session of questions and handed me a glass of acid green margarita. I don't know why, but I got a feeling it was an ordinary operation. After a couple of hours of soaking in the muddy bath, I was invited to Thanatos' chair.

"If the next answer is a lie, the electric nods in each diamond will perforate your cells with 40,000 volts," Mrs. Hydra explained sweetly.

"Why should I lie? I'm innocent."

"You lied that you are a doctor," she whispered. The eyes returned to life, and an unexpected rain of interrogative questions fell over me. During that procedure, the gang of strong soldiers appeared on my far left. They started to build something very similar to a guillotine.

"Do you agree with our Board's proposition?" Asked Judge Hydra. She was smiling and dancing, her belly covered in nasty sweat.

"I don't, and I do… Would you be so kind as to

repeat it? I've missed the last question because these men in the room distracted me," I sobbed.

"Did you know that Mrs. Sweet Hellfire was the artist behind the infinity sign on the napkins?" asked the angry voice from the humming eye above me.

"I didn't. Isn't she a dentist?"

"Yes, but that doesn't mean she can't draw… We do not allow this kind of discrimination in our town. Creativity is our birthright!"

For a moment, I lost control and couldn't figure out what was happening. I felt Mrs. Hydra's arms on my neck, then a chair transformed and softly embraced our two bodies. Every eye in the room watched us. I could feel a new bloom of heat in my already burning core.

"Of course, I do not argue with that," I staggered. I felt like a sneak, but my survival instinct—once more—swallowed the rest of my pride and honor.

"You know what I like about you? Your stuffed crab," Mrs. Hydra said, surprising me with the firm touch of her nails on my groin. Her eyes filled with lust as she welcomed my cheerful toy to her coral reef of salacity.

"Am I dreaming?" I muttered. My heart pounded like crazy; the chill of death was entirely gone.

We lay on the floor of red and green granite; our naked bodies occupied by sexual force. The floor-bed was wet and gentle, probably because that particular spot was reused more often than it should be. I was afraid that my name had been already erased from the minds of the Board and the body of Mrs. Hydra was some kind of consolation. It seemed logical… but to my surprise, the hatch in the floor had opened, and I fell down into the morning light where Medusa and Jellywobble were already waiting for me.

"You are cleared, Dr. Harmless. Congratulations! Here is a gift from the Board," said Jellywobble, the guard. He ceremonially led me to a bench under an elderberry tree, covered with sickly-smelling napkins. Under the tree, in a basket, rested a large nonvenomous (yellow) phyton.

"Her name is Miss Asunción; she just arrived from Southeast Africa. Mr. Alphonso Beard has ordered her for your needs as a companion."

"I hope she's tame," I mumbled.

"We don't know, and I wouldn't worry about that if I were you," Medusa, the second guard chuckled.

"I don't think doctors should have phytons as… hm, companions." I grabbed the nearest infinity napkin and covered my exposed 'gear' with it. My last words seemed to plunge the two young men into a gloomy silence.

"Miss Asunción is one hundred percent dedicated to the real friends of the Warrior Farm; that's all we know," Medusa explained.

"What does it mean?" I inquired nervously. The glare of four blank eyes didn't stop me. I grabbed the basket handle and said, "Okay, I see, I see… Some people got armadillos as their dedicated friends. Why not a deadly rock phyton in my case? After all, there're some things a man's just *gotta* have with a wife like mine. Or, perhaps, instead…"

beneath your feet

. . .

I WAS proud of the meeting results: it seemed I was cleared, and the murderer—whoever it was—had been identified. While walking through the city, I began whistling softly to myself. Ms. Asunción watched me from her basket, which I dragged behind me on the dusty road. People looked at me, the man covered in the red mud, with curiosity, but no one stopped to ask anything, and I began to forget that I was an enemy of this land (as well as the killer) just an hour ago.

"You are quite a celebrity here, Dr. Harmless," said the voice from the stairs. "Would you like to come in for a bite of fresh bread?

"How very kind of you, Mister...?"

"Everybody calls me FuzzyPie," he added, holding out his chubby hand to me.

I checked the gothic doors and signboard over the shop, carefully washed and gleaming in the sun, with the strange name on it: The Biscuit's Grave.

. . .

I picked the basket with a sleepy snake and, absurdly light-hearted, as though anything else mattered in the world, followed an odd man inside, where the smell of delicious homemade chicken pie came to my nostrils. What can I say? I'm only a human whom its hunger had again defeated.

Mr. FuzzyPie had a balding head with grey hair on the sides, combed neatly below his ears. He wore a floral shawl dropped over his waist. Despite my disappointment (I hoped to see a curvy young lady with pies in each hand), the man invited me to the unique bakery hall to "take a trip through time," as he explained it pushing me in.

The hall was dusty, with the scent of wet dogs and rainy summer. I noticed a wall with a beautiful drawing of Parthenon, a glowing hill against a night sky lit with stars, the constellation of the Apollon's Head (or the one and only Alphonso Beard), which was clearly visible above the eastern part of the room. Mr. FuzzyPie waved the remote control in his hand, and the illusion was gone.

Behind that wall with a drawing were all manner of weapons, blades— triangular and quadratic—axes, scissors, spoons, tools for gardening were arrayed on the desks, shelves, chairs, and plates. A boyish man of seventy-nine (or older) shouted, "Gee, one more… That should be fun!" Then he picked up a hefty ax blade, and I held my breath.

"Ah, my poor Mr. Harmless, I thought I'd never see you again," a sweet voice came from the depths of a hole dug in the middle of the room. It was Ms. Sedative and her crazy gang: Dinkie Dow, Blanca Speed, Spider Blue, Holly Terror, Candy de Beast, Tootsie Heavens, Peth Backwards, and Drowsy High. They sat near the hole in the floor, surrounded by the cheap tequila bottles, and smiled in solidarity. Ms. Sedative crawled out of the hollow opening and told me they planned to rob the bank across the road. She winked and added, "Mr. Alex Raphael hired me to do the job, but shhh... Alphonso's wolves don't know we are here."

"Hm, Alex Raphael didn't strike me as a criminal," I replied. "Well, what are you planning to steal? Cash, jewels, documents? I don't think it's possible. If you believe you can do it, then you all are too high or bonkers."

Ms. Sedative thought for a moment, then she pulled out a note from her Gadino bag (made of exotic crocodile skin, its clasp encrusted with thirty-nine white diamonds), lowered her voice and whispered, "We are planning to steal a safe deposit box #9. It's something very important..."

"Listen, you! I worked in Tanzania, Ethiopia, Stony Leak, and Black Beluga. I'm a Forrest Gump of the successful robbery, boy... While you were sucking your mom's tits, I was already running around killing for a living," yelled the boyish older man, smoking a cigar.

"There's an element of truth in his tales," Ms. Sedative chuckled, while chewing some green mushrooms. Then, she complained of exhaustion after a long working day—which was true enough—and said she had to take a nap. The rest of the crowd systematically dug the ground with their bare hands, completely forgetting about the helpful tools.

"I just wanted to remind you all of what can happen if Mr. Alphonso Beard finds out!" I said aloud.

"Shut up and eat your chicken pie!" I heard the bark behind the counter and was swept from the crowded circle into a lonely folding chair in the far corner. The physical discomfort had discouraged me from asking where my basket with Miss Asunción was. *It might be for the best if she got lost or ended up in the pie,* I sighed.

The late afternoon light filtered through the windows of The Biscuit's Grave bakery. Ms. Sedative and Mr. FuzzyPie shared the bottle of martini; their heads bowed toward each other. I giggled. As a result, Ms. Sedative handed me the rusted fork and ordered me to dig a new hole near the trash bin.

I asked her why on earth I had to do it if I didn't belong to their crew and got the clearest answer of all, "Because somebody has to do it, and that somebody is you, Bullet," she said. The boyish man with an ax helped bridge our views on the matter—I grabbed the fork from the floor and started to scoop like a madman.

To my amazement, the girls took a break again. They passed the pies, wine, olives, bread, and long sausages through the room, each of us—hardworking criminals—taking a bite. Our appetite woke up the maggots. Or, perhaps, they were activated by the heat in the room.

When Mr. FuzzyPie noticed the fresh worms around

my feet, his face shone, and he said proudly, "I usually mix them with sugar and bake them inside of the eyeballs you tried on the day of your arrival." He licked his lips and continued, "I buried 866 rats under this building, mostly to study. I was always fascinated by the ways nature recycled its dead and, of course, by the process of decomposition."

I groaned involuntarily after his horrific revelation but explained the howling sound by the stiffness in my limbs.

After a short calming meditation, I returned to my work. Suddenly, my bent fork stumbled upon a piece of dark blue cloth. I pulled the fabric, and after a few seconds, the sheriff's partially decayed female body appeared on the surface. The sick smell from the flesh rose like a powerful repulsing wave. I opened the window and looked outside in hopes of getting a breath of fresh air. Warrior Farm's military—the army, navy, air force, and special assistants in black suits with sophisticated guns was there in full force on the bakery's steps.

the wrath of wife

. . .

"WE ARE... NOT ALONE ANYMORE," I whispered the words, one-by-one.

Ms. Sedative stood up, came closer, and stuck her perfect body out of the window. She tilted her head, shook it from side to side like a wind-up toy, and, for a minute or two, blindly stared at the empty concrete steps. The army was gone.

"No one is there, silly!" She retrieved her slim figure from the window into the room and patted me on my shoulder. "It's hard to imagine a more cautious, even paranoid human being than you, Mr. Harmless. Lucky for us, Alphonso Beard is busy with his wedding preparation. Safety was our priority, and Mrs. Vegas promised she'd take care of it. Alex Raphael pays her $9,999 an hour, plus benefits."

"Quite a punishing job, but it has some pleasing rewards," Mr. FuzzyPie laughed.

I pretended I didn't hear his remark. After our short contact at the Meeting Hall and the promise to clean up my name, I tried to convince myself that Mrs. Vegas the Fifth was suffering to save me. The woman was an angel in the flesh, a messenger from Rsa; she was the person who united my crazy life in Gunung Kinabalu with my peaceful past, the spiritual with the physical, malignity with humanity.

I closed my eyes and turned 180 degrees on my toes, hoping that when I'd look out of the window, the army would be gone, but it wasn't. They stood there in silence, holding a digital poster: *How to Get Out Alive in Under One Minute*. The message had triggered hundreds of deadly scenarios inside of my mind. I ducked under the windowsill.

"We got a body to hide," Dinkie Dow and Tootsie Heavens alerted the stoned crowd of girls at the bottom of the closest pit. They agreed to help and began to crawl out toward the light. Without any warning, the boyish old man grabbed a couple of knives, switched on the music on his phone, and pushed the girls back: one-by-one. His dangerous 'dancing with knives' caused an imbalance, and he dropped the phone below the ground. The music didn't stop. Carefully, I tiptoed to the pit, soaking in every word of the strange song:

I'm in the block where you can't go in
Yeah, bro, you feel that?
Smokin' that gas, can you hear that?
Loud pack, ooh, it's that loud pack
Smokin' that anthrax
In that Maybach, yeah, we kick back
Hoes just say wanna suck that
I know that they love that...

I can't explain what happened after, but it was over very quickly: the men outside reached for their weapons; the stream of heavy bullets knocked against the bakery wall; the girls jumped out, hooting and whistling like bandits. The men in black killed them in less than a second.

"Ha! They know their business," Ms. Sedative rolled over to me and sat up. She unbuttoned her top and asked if I'd mind sharing my jizz with her for the last time. I couldn't decide what to do: it was too good to be true... I could hardly breathe, afraid to spook her unexpected desire to die while giving me the last minutes of pleasure on Earth. Ms. Sedative grabbed my wilted penis, and I prepared to pump the rest of my energy onto her welcoming arms, but at that moment, I saw Mr. FuzzyPie's face between her legs. Then, all I remembered was a squawking noise in the background; how my head ached (probably the result of overworking); how the windows shattered; how the door banged left and right as the special force in black filled all visible space in the room. Not for too long.

Soon enough, the roof burst into flames. Ms. Sedative's wild cry followed the sound of the explosion. I bounced to my feet, looking for Mr. FuzzyPie. He was nowhere to be seen. *That bastard is a real demon. He had slipped away; I'm sure he's got a hidden place here*! I thought. I was wrong. Mr. FuzzyPie used the chaos to sneak unnoticed into the bank and steal safe box: #9.

There was blood everywhere: mainly from the sweet knocked out girls, as well as the stench of burning flesh from the boyish old man and 866 rats' bodies—a delightful bakery transformed into a butcher's shop. Ms. Sedative stood behind the ruins of the bar, pouring tequila straight into her mouth. Her hands shook.

The man in black went in and yelled, "Doctor Harmless, your wife called us to find and deliver you home safely for supper!"

I staggered and jiggled; a harsh laugh escaped my dry lips.

"All this because my wife wanted to see me? For supper? And who are you?"

"We are Sierras Find & Kill Guyamas, we are the delivery force. Today, we had to ask for reinforcements from Alphonso Beard's army because we got an anonymous call about the planned bank robbery across the road. Did you hear anything about it, doctor?" a face, entirely covered in a black mask, asked.

I glanced at the underground chambers and tunnels, a pile of sand behind him, forming a large mound near each pit. Bewildered by the question, I turned to Ms. Sedative, who was just as shocked as I was, snapped my fingers, and said, "Give me that bottle, quickly! Or anything!"

home, sweet home

. . .

THE SIERRAS FIND & Kill Guyamas team forced me inside the bulletproof van to deliver my body safely to the destination. My tired bones swayed from side to side as if penetrated by the speed and annoyance of the rumbling wheels of our car. It seemed the men in black masks enjoyed their trip; they were superbly indifferent to my aches and troubles. I shook my head and shrugged my shoulders violently, telling them with my eyes the things that I could never say in words. My mind was churning with endless questions: *What have I done to deserve a hunt like this? Is my time on this planet almost up? What have I failed at? What is the outcome of my life?*

A source of my angry speech sat across from me and chewed on his grilled larvae stuffed with pumpkin and potato mush. My empty stomach began to purr the tune of starvation. The melody of heavy drops of rain made contact with the van's roof and muffled the sound of my constant hunger.

My attention switched when we made a sudden stop and the boys carried me out to the castle's doors. When they left, I stood up and, without hesitation, jangled the gold bell that hung outside. The delicious aroma of pudding promised an incredible celebration of my arrival.

No one opened. Anxious, I pushed the door and stepped out of the darkness into the light of the cozy hall. A mysterious, visibly unhappy, but beautiful woman in a white dress looked straight at me.

"Who are you?" I asked, scratching my arms nervously.

"What? What is all this nonsense?" the woman barked. "I'm your wife! What's wrong with you, Mr. Harmless?"

A laugh began to rise in my throat but stopped abruptly. I noticed a half-naked figure of Alex Raphael with a mouth full of pudding. He came in through the living room door located in the castle's heart: too relaxed, somewhat sparkling, slowly pulling on his trousers.

Alex Raphael glanced at me, muttered something to the woman, then pushed her back through the door to the closest bedroom. He wiped the sweat from his forehead and came forward.

"She is Mrs. Sweet Hellfire but in transformation. I'm her first husband, the real one, the one everybody thinks is dead. Let me explain, Bullet… I was happy, healthy, enjoyed my life to the fullest, and worked as the Head of the Medical Center on the Warrior Farm. When LKED was discovered in our female population, I was the first to suggest the perfect solution, the only one who designed the cure to save the lives of thousands of innocent people. But the Board refused to believe me. The cure was stolen from my laboratory a month ago. After that, Alphonso Beard staged my death and made me disappear forever. Thanks to King Hamilton, I've got one more chance to fight for what I think is right."

"Is that so...?" I responded. A sick feeling of a new fake drama crept into my heart; I squeezed my eyes to focus on the man's face.

"The change is constant" Alex Raphael continued, "so as far as I know, it is only happening once a week, but according to the latest data and my calculations, the LKED plague is going to accelerate with time."

"Do you mean that my—hm, our wife, is going to look different next week? Do you mean I won't recognize her again?"

"Exactly! Just imagine what damage it could do to our brains, as well as our society, if the change accelerates rapidly!"

"What if your LKED plague is true *hope* for everybody on this planet? Just imagine: no matter where you are in life, you can change... I mean, it gives you the chance to switch your appearance and start living the life you deserve to live."

"Maybe you are right, Dr. Harmless... Still, it might be very challenging, especially when you lose the connection with people you know, respect, and love. They'd see you as a stranger; it would take time to re-establish relationships, but then, wait...you'd suddenly change again. And again! I've also noticed that the change shifts between the low and the grand, between the ugly and the gorgeous."

I stood and quietly listened to him. I was perplexed by the news and his passionate lecture: it was as if this was happening to someone else, not me.

"Why did you want to rob the bank?" I changed the topic of conversation.

"To get bacteriophage."

"Who?"

"It's a bacteria eater," Alex Raphael clarified with a weak smile.

There was a reasonably heavy silence, because after all the bombing and beating, my cells refused to work at full capacity. While thinking, I subconsciously walked into the dining room, grabbed a piece of delicious pudding from the table, found a glass, and filled it with an eye-shattering, glowing drink from a jug cooling in a bucket of ice.

"It's only a virus that infects bacteria and destroys the cells of the host. It's absolutely harmless," Alex Raphael whispered from behind.

"Wait, stop! I don't get it. What is LKED really: bacterial disease or virus?"

"Both. It's a hybrid."

His explanation wasn't soothing. For a moment, I thought if I moved quick enough, I'd knock him on the floor without any difficulty. Then, I'd push the button on the wall, get into the library, and hide there until Alphonso Beard's army came and saved me.

"Don't worry, Alex. We'll talk some sense into him

later," someone chirped from the hall. I recognized the voice of the first assistant: he was dressed in a blue silk shirt open at the neck and gigantic blue glasses. I admired his ability to sneak into any house in the Warrior Farm, but I saw a real danger in his elephantine, meaty belly this time.

"I've heard you are familiar with the voodoo concept," the first assistant smiled, reaching out for the pudding.

"Am I? Well, if you say so…" In a flash, I stuffed my mouth with the last two pieces on the table.

The first assistant frowned and pouted his lips like a little child. "Mrs. Vegas told me to bring you to survey her new bedroom for demonic or malign presences and to ensure that the design itself, as well as the placement of her bed, is propitious and safe."

I agreed to help. I was forever in debt to the fabulous Mrs. Vegas the Fifth.

On the way to the door, I gazed back one more time, detecting the expression of fury in my wife's eyes, and added mildly, "It was a divine pudding, Mrs. Sweet Hellfire!"

She ignored my mention. Her eyes, cold enough to freeze the marrow in my bones, were the answer I was looking for: she hoped I would never get back from that short voodoo-trip.

"I need to clear my head anyway. I won't be long," I said to Alex Raphael sadly, observing how Mrs. Sweet Hellfire dropped to her knees, how her soft fingers brushed against his skin, how her hungry mouth ripped open his trousers.

I swallowed a howl, and surrendering to the arms of fate, followed the first assistant out. It was nearly night (or morning?): the garden was in shadows; the trees were still. For some reason, I was filled with the most terrible feeling of loneliness I have ever known.

"Would you believe me, Mr. Harmless, if I told you I was 'almost married' once too?" the first assistant broke the silence. "Ah, I still remember it as if it was yesterday! I was trained for our yearly sin marathon, but then I met Mr. SingleShot, and…"

"Please, stop. I believe you; you certainly have a convincing enough look… Hm, I'd marry you, too, if my name were Mr. SingleShot," I joked.

He looked back at me over his shoulder, then turned and took my hand in his. "Let's do it, Mr. Harmless. We could all be dead by 9:99 a.m. anyway."

While I mumbled a prayer to God to give me the patience to explain that I can't marry every person I meet, I caught a strange glimpse of his fingers, pulling something big and glossy from his jeans in a quite leisurely fashion…

It was only Miss Asunción!

the one minute happiness

. . .

WE CROSSED the river from the gates into the main street. The road on the other side of the town was reasonably broad, and well-lit but crowded for that time of the night. At first glance, everything seemed normal: birds chanted in sweet, so-recognizable disharmony; a couple of ladies were shedding their skins and faces on the go; the sky was full of the unicorn-flies. *But something wasn't normal. Or someone.*

In the middle of the path, surrounded by a dozen wild dogs, stood the woman: short, angry, and not young. When I noticed a revolver in her hand, I immediately dismissed the idea that she was a destination tourist or an unlucky visitor like myself. What was even odder was that she was carrying an empty can of coke on her neck, about the size of a small kettle; every now and then, she raised it and seemed to speak into it.

I pulled my shoulders back and whispered to the startled first assistant, "Who is the woman with the gun?"

"I'm not sure... A friend of mine mentioned her once," he said, puzzled.

"My name is Tamara GRRR Diablo Thrill of the Balance de Razor Perditis Yo Legarto," the woman shouted, her cobalt-colored lips tightened over her smoke-orange teeth.

"I'm Bullet. Is it your dogs, Mrs. GRRR?" I sucked the air in, inspecting her muscles under her tight top.

"Yes. I imported them a while ago. They are New Guinea Singing dogs." She paused, then added, "It's important I speak with you, fellas."

"What did you say your name was?" The first assistant said in a high-pitched voice, edged with fear, from behind my back.

"Tamara GRRR Diablo Thrill of the Balance de Razor Perditis Yo Legarto, or, if you want to simplify, I am the third wife of Mr. Beard."

"Right," the first assistant sighed. In that exact second, an unpleasant change had come over his face: his jaw dropped slightly; his cheeks changed color to the dark, muted cyan; he was breathing rather quickly like he was frightened. I kept darting sidelong glances at him while listening to a stranger with the dogs.

"I specialize in the future, Bullet. Before I discuss the matter, let me ask you, and it is of the most vicious importance, to sign a non-disclosure agreement. It will take only one minute."

"Future, you say… hm, like five years from now?" I tried to bide some time to find the best way to escape the crazy situation.

"Five, twenty. Or 200."

"I'll be dead by then, Mrs. GRRR. What do I need a non-disclosure for?"

"I'm not trying to fool you, Bullet," she smiled. Her pose and expression suggested she was irritated by my sudden disobedience. "I work for Mrs. Fairly Breathing, the first wife of the ruler of this land."

I saw how the first assistant put his hands on his throat, almost hysterical terror took over him.

"Would you like to take a closer look at the paper's content in my lounge down the rock, Mr. Harmless?" the woman continued.

"Before we do that, I think I need to visit the soon-to-be wife of your ex-husband," I chuckled.

"I'll shoot you down if you try to leave now. Understood?" Mrs. GRRR barked.

I realized she was waiting for my response. Despite my stiff body, I moved closer to the edge of the road, only to discover the steep rock wall, and peered over. There was a long chain of stairs leading down to the lounge, which was covered in lights. I opened my mouth to answer, but the words resisted coming out of my throat. I glanced back to ask for the first assistant's advice. One of the wild dogs sat on his chest, pressing on his lungs, stifling him. Deep in my heart, I wanted to scream that I was ready to follow Mrs. GRRR to the end of the Earth, but my conscious brain had lost control of my tongue. I gasped out only a single word, "No."

I don't know how, but the first assistant, red and hot, planted himself in the center of the road, waving his arms and eyeballs impatiently for a better effect; he tried to scare away the dogs, or perhaps, attract the attention of people who lived nearby. Mrs. GRRR Diablo Thrill of the Balance de Razor Perditis Yo Legarto spat on her hands, then quickly approached the first assistant and gave him a hard blow with her can of coke. Pale-faced I watched that operation in silence. The collision made a mess on the road where the first assistant stood only a couple of minutes ago. I bravely decided to break the mournful silence and jump from the edge of the wall. The dogs (after taking me into the ring) followed my unplanned voyage.

Mrs. GRRR came down to the lounge peacefully by using the stairs. There she checked my wounds (I admit, I was lucky enough to survive the rough two-meter flight) and got right down to business. After I'd signed the non-disclosure, the crazy dog lady told me that she had a vision: after the wedding, Mr. Beard was planning to send my poor soul to the Slave Market, where I'd be sold to the Beluga Clan. I was confused by that information. She smiled, turned her head toward the egg hammock, and spoke in a low, cheerful voice, "Your ex-wife, Martha, said you can give me one minute of happiness."

A sudden horror pierced my body like an arrow. The thought of being together with Mrs. GRRR on that egg hammock caused every limb of my body to shiver. I grabbed the bottle of locally made gin, which I spotted on the three-legged table in the corner, and growled,

"What does your Martha know? In my world, one minute is an eternity!"

After a minute (or two) of speedy action, I felt dead in more ways than one. I found myself staggering, perhaps, because I had eaten only two meals that day and could not remember the last time I had slept properly. Also, I was furious with the fatigue-clumsiness of my usually mighty anaconda as well as the slowness of my body. It seemed that Mrs. GRRR was tired, too. She and her eleven New Guinea Singing dogs fell asleep under the table overshadowed by the stone wall. A wet, monotonous wind healed my wounds quicker than any first aid kit. I needed a rest, too, so I crawled into a hole in the floor and closed my eyes.

The following day, I found Tamara's body—eyeless and cold— professionally strangled and placed on the stairs. A plate of cold ham and a napkin was left on the three-legged table. The New Guinea Singing dogs were gone.

"I might call myself Pompeii after that," I said to myself, enjoying the sound of the echo.

I couldn't decide the wisest thing to do, so I climbed up to the road and prowled the unknown streets for a quarter of an hour in hopes of finding the bride's castle. When I thought the search was a waste of time, I noticed a peculiar smell. It led me directly to Mrs. Vegas's palace.

Quite courteously, I opened the door with my foot. Above the French doors that framed the entrance were hung twelve dead sheep and forty-two living fish. On the other side of the room, stood a half-naked Mrs. Vegas. Her glowing body was a page waiting to be read.

the qi attack

. . .

IT WAS A LONG CORRIDOR—A room where anything could happen on the way to the object of your desires. It had a narrow entry, approximately 300 meters long that gradually decreased in size, then turned into a small tight tunnel. I waved to Mrs. Vegas's sweet silhouette, nervously waiting at the other end.

I began the trip in her direction, carefully avoiding open doors, dark corners, and unwanted erotic encounters. The closer I got to the stairs, the more I could feel the power of Qi on my skin. All the space around me disappeared. I found myself facing the bride's trembling, itchy, and burning legs on the golden stairs. Only then did I allow myself to open my mind and give the green light to a continuous flow of energy in my lower body.

I drank her in; her swaying hips and lean legs, unaware of the ecstasy they caused just by existing on this planet. *What would happen if I licked them?* I thought.

"Nothing," Mrs. Vegas said.

It seemed I asked the question (which circled in my brain the last couple of minutes) aloud.

"I thought you liked it when I did it last time, in Rsa," I said, offended by her remark.

"I did. But just because I liked it *then* doesn't mean I like it every time, Bullet."

After these words, without allowing me to comprehend them, she grabbed my hand and dragged me up the golden stairs. Everything happened so fast that I came to my senses only when in front of the red door.

Her bedroom was full of people: some held thick advertising booklets in their hands, others spoke on the phones—sweat dripped from their faces. Ms. Asunción snored peacefully on the chair without a single sign of worry: her breakfast, lunch, and dinner were together in one place. How convenient! That idea made me cringe.

Twelve sheep and forty-two fishes—the present from the future husband, Mr. Beard—were carefully brought in into the room from the hall. It turned out that Mr. Beard was convinced that such a gesture would bring much happiness and harmonize the energy on the wedding night.

"You have to find that damn Qi, Bullet. I don't know how, but you have to find it; otherwise, that demon, Mr. Beard, will cancel the wedding, and I'll lose my boy, who is currently in the clutches of a cruel mad ruler of Beluga Clan," Mrs. Vegas cried.

She told me, confidentially, how she followed her husband and Mr. Killing to Gunung Kinabalu and how her son—only because of his naïve curiosity—killed (again!) the sacred frog, the favorite animal of the local shaman.

I glanced at the bed and nodded, "Let me help you!" The bed was placed perfectly in the command position and facing the entry door. In Feng Shui, it is one of the most private places in the home. We spend a great amount of time there, often in an unconscious state. My next stop was near the orange curtains. The Qi color of the season was poppy sunset—bright reds melting in the sky as summer makes its exit—the color was soothing to the nerves.

"What are you doing? Are you even listening?" Mrs. Vegas was irritated by my sluggish movements.

"Shhh, I'm absorbing the Qi of your bedroom."

I noticed that people had left the room, and we were alone in the middle of it. At that moment, a shadow behind the window caught my attention. After a couple of weeks of uncertainty, dealing with crimes and lustful women, I couldn't make out who it was, but it had the shape of a square and was wearing what looked like a lamp on its head. Confused, I stopped and slowly reached for the vase on the nearest nightstand. The silhouette appeared before I could strike.

"Do you have a friend over?" I asked Mrs. Vegas as carefully as possible.

"Ah, that… just Auntie Cactus. She came over to help with the Qi."

"I love decorating, Mister. I think this room needs more prickly plants." The woman from behind the curtain grunted, then cleared her throat and continued,

"I'm still not sure about the bed, but I think if I could try it out for an hour or so."

"Please, without me!" I squealed, but it didn't help.

After the longest hour of my life, I sat up, feeling the bed still wobbling beneath me. The door opened, and Mr. Vegas's curious head appeared in the doorway.

"What's the matter, dear Auntie Cactus? You look so downcast!" Mr. Beard's future wife exclaimed.

"A friend of mine died this morning," Auntie Cactus said, while tears appeared and then dried instantly on her face.

"Oh, no. Who?"

"His name was Ale de Sandwich, known to the world as the first assistant," Auntie Cactus explained.

"You poor, poor thing. Do you know what I think? I think you need a little bit more time with Mr. Harmless," Mrs. Vegas winked. Her positivity, empathy, and desire to help were contagious. "What do you say, Bullet? One more time?"

"Maybe. Maybe," I muttered, looking at the exquisite porcelain figure of the hippopotamus in the far corner. I tried to estimate the weight of this figurine by the eye—*how heavy was it?*

"Ah, that would be a wonderful Qi service. Almost like Sunday shopping," Auntie Cactus cackled.

"Good luck, you two. Don't scare the Qi away!" Mrs. Vegas laughed and closed the door. Then, the unthinkable happened. Auntie Cactus stepped over to the bed, spread her legs, and jumped on my back.

"Brighten up my Qi, Bullet!" she commanded.

I had to take a few breaths before answering, "At first, I have to detoxify the surrounding area and maybe even get rid of some poisonous elements inside my aura."

"Do it, boy! Now! Or I'll tell Mr. Beard that you are the reason the Qi is gone from Gunung Kinabalu!" the words suffocated her. Suddenly, Auntie fell to her side and started to choke.

Her message startled me but also awoke some guilt. After all, I was here as a doctor; I was supposed to help to find the Qi in the room. With difficulty, I turned Auntie Cactus on her back and began analyzing her purple wrinkles. With sadness in my heart, I realized that she was still alive.

"May I touch it?" she opened her eyes and placed her hand on my *silent spindle*.

"Yes."

One hour… one minute… one second. The ceiling. The Qi sat beside me on the bed, listening to my anxious breathing.

"Thank God it is over! It is over… The Qi is here!" I whispered.

"I'm still a bit hungry," Auntie Cactus mumbled. "Would you mind repeating?"

Almost automatically, I wiped off the sweat, picked up my bitter but brave *spindle* covered in lavender-tinted hair, and began a new dance on a glossy bed. I guess my body demanded that I partake of this demonic feast laid out before me.

• • •

After the third time, I felt exhausted. I heard how Auntie Cactus got up, slid her steel-dry feet into slippers, cleaned out the nightstand table, then pushed the panel behind the window to the right, stepped into the darkness, and jogged down the invisible stairs.

Why are you still here, Bullet? Run. Run. Run. My mind spoke to me.

"No. I can't go without finding Qi!" I said to myself aloud.

The emptiness sighed back. On the blue screen above the bed appeared young and blonde Ms. Break de Roof, with a familiar box #9 in her hands.

"What do you want? What is there?" I shouted, the blood freezing in my veins.

"Bacteriophages. Mr. Fuzzy Pie told me to leave it for you with a message, 'Find Tamara GRRR or Alexander Raphael; they know what to do with it,'" the young woman with smooth olive skin and provocative grey eyes said.

"Anything else?" I hissed. I hated my life at that moment.

"Hm… it was kind of impressive. I mean you and Auntie Cactus. It was her birthday today—forty-five years old," Ms. Break de Roof paused.

"Forty-five? No way! She looked like she had arrived from the Kingdom of the Dead, the sunless place, the underworld… Is she sick with LKED?"

"No, silly… She wasn't wearing makeup, that's all," the second assistant explained with displeasure in her voice. "By the way, at the end… I didn't get what is 'the

Qi Attack.' You shouted it pretty often during the last session."

"That's not your business!"

"We have an excellent clinic in…"

"Piss off, de Roof!"

"Just wanted to help, Mr. Harmless."

The screen went blue again. I sat, hugged my knees, and started to weep.

in the teeth of lost memory

. . .

DO *you remember the words of Henry Miller? "Life's wildest moment—she kneels on the sidewalk. Everything else she does is lies, lies, lies." This is how I felt—used by every woman I've met so far, especially by Mrs. Vegas.*

Did I find Qi, or did I not? That, my friend, is the tricky question. All I could remember was a sensation of the night on my skin, and Ms. Break de Roof with a satisfied chuckle on her face, dressed like a surgeon in the middle of a critical operation, repeating, "Clamp with II, clear with III, breathe in on my count... Mrs. Vegas, we can lose him at any time."

Just the thought of that conversation made me shiver like a leaf. And then, suddenly, Auntie Cactus's voice came from behind the curtain, "Poor doc, you should give him an injection of prussic acid, darling. Or anything, really." Her harsh and ugly cynicism was the last thing I remembered about the day I visited Mrs. Vegas's palace.

Now, let me tell you, I don't know how it feels to be

unconscious, but I sure know how it feels to be wet. When I opened my eyes, I was lying in the bathtub, naked, with a mask on my face, razor in hand and an expensive watch on. I bent forward, found a towel, and with a small sigh of relief, began to examine the room. Three doors, five windows. *What happened? And which door is the way out of this hell?*

The middle door opened. A big woman with a pink nose dressed as a queen approached my bath and, with a mellow smile, like an intoxicated flute, announced, "Hullorr, Mista Beeard! I'm so glad I found you arrlive."

All right, all right, don't worry. Just close your eyes and count to five—she'll be gone.

"Who are you?" I asked after a few hasty breaths.

"Ms. Divine Madness, a special agent of Cut & Infect. You might have trouble remembering me; you crashed from the third floor last night."

The pictures of yesterday arrived in some kind of broken vision board quality: at first, the blue screen had fallen on my head but didn't kill me; then, I heard Mrs. Vegas and the second assistant's whispers, who spoke about "moving the body," "nobody could ever know because nobody has ever seen his face," "he might have died, anyhow, of shock, after the night with Auntie Cactus," and at the end, the memory of the giant iron hippopotamus that had been thrown at me by Mr. Beard's blurred shadow.

As the bathroom atmosphere thickened with panic and despair, Ms. Divine Madness became increasingly aware that I needed help safely getting out of the bath.

She slipped one hand into the water and opened her glittering dress with another. It wasn't just the raw desire that surged through my body in that second, it was the feeling of power. Every cell of me blazed with thirst. But talking with a special agent is not always easy… After all, the woman was six-feet-three plus, broad and strong in proportion.

"Would you like us to do a postmortem?" Ms. Divine Madness asked.

"With whom?"

"With Mr. Harmless. He died in your bed yesterday. Your soon-to-be wife, Mrs. Vegas, told us that he finally found Qi, which ended his life. So tragic!"

I coughed. "I think I remember that name. Please, he doesn't need a postmortem; Mr. Harmless has suffered enough."

"What an amazing perrrsona you are, Mr. Beaard! The kindest governor everrr! You know the storrrry of every visitor in our town, don't you? You really do care," the big woman chirped in my ear.

No, I didn't care. My hands twitched, screaming to run themselves over those luscious shoulders, to slide my tongue into her wet orifice, to touch the curves of her muscular waist. My sleepy *spindle* woke up and began to drool with anticipation, dreaming of entering her athletically built fountain of passion.

After a couple of minutes, I dropped to the floor, exhausted by an incredible speed of the special agent from Cut & Infect.

"I admire your speed qualities, Ms. Divine Madness! But I have to rush home… I mean, to visit the widow of

Mr. Harmless. She's probably wondering what's happened to her husband… and I have to visit the clinic. Soon. Today… Now? We must save as many victims of LKED as possible!"

"Ah, I envy how your mind works—pure brilliance. But don't be too naïve; you can't save them all. And it's absurd that you have to do this kind of thing—visiting widows, listening to their cries, feeding their hungry mouths. You are the king, not a slave. Don't you have an assistant for that?"

"What an idiot I am!" I laughed nervously. "Of course, I can send Ms. Break de Roof. Still, I'd like to end the problem with LKED. What about the modern research of that fellow, mmm… Alexander Raphael?"

"What? You hated him! He was a strange man… not that smart, though, because he ended up dead. You hired my arrr-gency to kill him."

"Right. Of course, I did," I trembled in disgust.

The most remarkable thing about my *spindle* is that it never listens. It makes its own decisions: such as rubbing itself over every inch of Ms. Divine Madness's belly while I spoke to her. Yes, I was tired; I needed to sleep very badly, but all I did (like the dumb doll) was restlessly pull Ms. Divine Madness's hips closer and closer to me. Finally, I gave up! I pressed myself against her ripe dates and slid my greedy *spindle* between her thighs. *Ah, what a feeling! Let's do it again!*

Suddenly, it all stopped. The bride of the house, somewhat astonished, stood in the doorway. She produced a sharp knife from her pocket and furiously asked Ms. Divine Madness to leave the room immediately.

"You are a monster! Today is our wedding!" Mrs. Vegas groaned once the half-naked special agent had left the bedroom.

I shifted restlessly upon pillows on the floor.

"If I have rightly understood, we aren't married yet. Well, I suggest that..."

"I didn't mean it; all I just said, Bu...," Mrs. Vegas paused. "Ha, I don't seem able to think normally today; I forget things and go blank for hours, darling Beard. Don't you?"

Her sweet voice alarmed me, but I nodded.

"A wife is not a structure of bones, who follows house rules and serves delicious sex each night, but a wish, a dream, a tiger behind bars, or all of these together!" Mrs. Vegas pressed herself against me. I knew I was being offered a dangerous gift—her two witchy, perky balloons were looking straight at my face, telling me, "we know what you want, go ahead, take us."

But something inside me screamed, *be careful with this irrational, kooky woman*. Mrs. Vegas's eyes gravitated toward the towel; her itchy longing was affecting me, too. I swallowed my suspicion, pretended I lost my memory, and accepted the bride in my arms.

the other martha

. . .

THE BLUE SCREEN'S jangling melody woke me up. I cleared my throat, expecting to hear the second assistant's voice, then rolled over Mrs. Vegas's flawless, naked body, who opened one eye to see if I was trying to run away from my morning duties.

"Ms. Break de Roof? I asked.

The new blue screen lit up, and the familiar face of my personal enemy number one, Arcadio, appeared above me, smiling. He was standing outside, surrounded by long-haired nymphs of different sizes and shapes with cocktails in their hands, moving to the beat of the demonic music in the background.

"We need to talk to you, Alphonso," he said. Behind him Captain Happy danced and sipped on a beer. I noticed that he spoke to someone behind the screen and giggled.

"Hey, fellas," I responded royally after a short pause. "Why are you in such a hurry? Come over to my wedding and we'll discuss your problems."

"I think we need to meet up before the wedding, Mr. Beard, as a matter of some urgency," Arcadio insisted.

"Legal urgency? Maybe my assistant can help you."

"I don't think so… You know someone who knows someone who might know someone who knows someone we can't find right now."

"Well, if that someone's got a beautiful smile, I'm all in," I exclaimed with a note of superior dominance.

We agreed to meet outside. After a long fitting, I finally chose the perfect suit and stepped into the light, satisfied with my appearance. Behind the door, I faced a queue of strangers discussing the details of the sudden death of Mr. Harmless and the current problems between the Beluga Clan and the Warrior Farm. I wanted to join their discussion, but the second assistant pulled me out through the tunnel and shoved me into a black car.

The car delivered my royal body to the door of palace #77. I rang, expecting to see my beautiful widow. I was annoyed to be met with the woman who opened the door, because her face was utterly unfamiliar to me —it seemed LKED was spreading at the speed of light in this country. I explained my early, unscheduled visit shortly.

"Ah, my poor, poor angel, Bullet. To turn a healthy, smart, strong man into a piece of rotten flesh is what our kingdom does best," cried Mrs. Sweet Hellfire.

"I'm not sure if you are aware of it, but I'm representing the kingdom, my dear," I said, convincing myself that I had to play along.

"I just lost my husband," Mrs. Sweet Hellfire

shouted. "Give me a bit of peace, will you? I need to do some grieving today, Mr. Beard."

"Right, then I'll leave you alone," I said, taking a quick last look around—no lights in the rooms, no sign of cherry cake in the kitchen. Yes, Alexander Raphael was gone.

"It's a bit of a spacious house for one person, though," I continued. "Maybe you want to do something about it. It's your choice; either you'll stay here and spend quality time with your king, or you can risk going back to the woods."

Her crying stopped. She stretched her long, milky arms and pushed me toward an empty chair near the exit door. The meaning of her next move was loud and clear.

"Let me skip foreplays, my king!" She growled and stripped down my trousers. Her dominant tone sent shivers down my spine.

When Mrs. Sweet Hellfire fit my entire *spindle* inside her cave, I crawled down and began to guide her in the best direction. She looked above me for the last time and asked, "Hm, what is your driver doing here?"

I glanced back. Just as I remembered him, the one and only Captain Happy stood in the day's sunlight. His expression was mischievous; I couldn't tell how long he'd been here.

"*That* just made me a little jealous, Mr. Beard," Captain Happy whispered through his teeth.

I laughed nervously. "I'm not sure what you saw. We were just trying to figure out how to continue with our lives after the death of our beloved friend, Mr. Harmless."

"I liked the intensity… I think… last time I felt this kind of intensity was in a random bathroom with Martha."

It took sixty-two seconds before the image of Martha, my ex-wife, and Captain Happy sank in and expanded in my chest.

"When was that exactly?" I asked suspiciously.

My always-ready-to-fight *spindle* was ripped from the pleasure of discovering the dark corners of Mrs. Sweet Hellfire, who willingly surrendered to my charms. I was also disappointed, but I couldn't stop myself from learning the truth about Martha's betrayal.

"A couple of years ago. Through her mother. Didn't I tell you all that when we started to plan our *game*?"

I knew those words would haunt me forever. I was lured to the distant land of killers, stupid idlers, and mad addicts by the woman I trusted most.

Mrs. Sweet Hellfire's reaction wasn't quite what I had expected. She adjusted the chair, lay flat on her back, and welcomed her new guest.

"Hey, it's almost the afternoon," I mumbled. Then, I pulled Captain Happy's smelly jacket over my head as a cover and sat in the middle of the corridor for about an hour or so. I listened to Captain Happy's satisfied roar and wondered what the hell had gone wrong (again), what I could do next, and where all my seven leggy servants were.

Tired of waiting, I collapsed on the floor, still haunted by Captain Happy's confession about Martha's involvement in my current situation. Mrs. Sweet Hellfire's lewd sounds made me grit my teeth harder. I saw how she arched her back, giving Captain Happy total access to her surprisingly stretchy playground. The floor began to shake, and her first scream, "the storm is hereeee!" changed my seating position… I gripped my *spindle* and prayed they'd continue for a while. *For a while* lasted for hours.

When the three of us lay quietly on the floor, staring at each other, I sighed. "I have something planned for this evening, Mrs. Sweet Hellfire, but after my wedding night, I'm absolutely free."

Captain Happy smirked. "We need to go now, Alphonso. Martha and Arcadio are waiting in the Medical Center."

"What? No way, I'm not going," I grunted. Captain Happy didn't listen. He took my left hand and dragged me out to his funny, orange car.

This kingdom is fucking with my head, I said to myself. *Look at your life, King Bullet…*

The rusty door of the neurological facility of the famous Medical Center opened, and four people with outstretched arms welcomed me into the giant, never-ending courtyard. The place smelled of cigarettes and grease; a hundred benches nearly as long as a railway station stood near the dirty walls, and broken windows were covered with a purple sheet. On the right side of the entrance stood a built-in seventy-nine percent alcohol machine.

As it turned out, only two people, Dr. Constanza Lovesick and her half-brother Bip SoBelt ran the center. While holding hands, they kneeled before me with a smile. Behind them was Arcadio's silhouette (without his beloved Jack) and a tall woman of exceptional beauty hanging frivolously on his right shoulder.

"Would you introduce me to your lady?" I asked him after we shook hands.

"This is Martha. Her third version, after she was infected with LKED."

"Is… it… so?" I almost choked on my own saliva.

"Yeah, beautiful, but still like rat poison. Be careful, Alphonso!" Captain Happy whispered in my ear. "She forced Bip SoBelt to marry her yesterday."

"How?"

"I don't know. Some are saying it was at gunpoint; others, she fed him ackee fruit and he almost died."

My *spindle* woke up. Perhaps, he was trying to remind me that he was in charge, and all he could think about was getting the woman, who stood and laughed near Arcadio, in his bed. I didn't care about the reason. I simply agreed with him.

passing through difficulties

. . .

DO you remember how the Dalai Lama once said that you could be a rich and powerful man, with a big house and a huge bedroom playing relaxing music, but still be full of jealousy, anger, and attachment and unable to relax? I was that man. Becoming Alphonso Beard destroyed my peace of mind. All I ever wanted was to be free—*a wandering rebellious spirit looking for the love of his life*—unchained from the constant judgment of small minds of Rsa, independent and unconquered, a symbolic and cultured figure, or let's say, a simple genius of some kind. Any kind.

Did I want too much?

Instead, especially after becoming Alphonso, all I felt was emptiness and danger. That danger followed me everywhere: first, through hundreds of perfect bodies and smiles, and later, from every dark gateway or unfamiliar face, phrase, and word that I did not understand or could not understand. "There are worse crimes than pretending to be someone else, Bullet," you'd say. I know. But when it was all delivered on a golden plate, I just wanted a simple bed and a picture of Margaret Thatcher in my hand.

Constant quarrels with my three wives—let's call them fear, stress, and anxiety—removed me further and further from my so-desired peace and relaxation. My daily sex life improved, but my *spindle,* usually happy, humming, and spinning with bright colors, developed issues after being surrounded by the crazy women day and night. It probably was not suited to the large and noisy activities of the Warrior Farm. Then, there was the feeling of being constantly observed, making it impossible to chill without provoking another chain of sexual games with anxious or deadly endings.

Constanza Lovesick gently pushed me into a damp room with narrow rusty beds and torn bedspreads, which naturally interrupted my gloomy thoughts. A sixth sense—if I ever had any—tried to warn me after she locked the door.

"I understand you are a busy man… Ah, my marriage was the most wonderful thing that ever happened to me, Mr. Beard, so I know how you feel today. All those dreams!" she sighed and continued. "But we have to ask you for more money for our little magical clinic."

"There's no rush, Miss Lovesick. Let me have my dreams," I said, noticing a big gummy bat in her hand, beautiful in its simplicity, capturing so much light from the window in just a few straight lines.

"In our job, dreaming can be a dangerous thing. We sell health, help, mmm… pills. Look around and see for yourself: we need more resources for the advanced research we are currently conducting. Fifteen thousand souls are crying for your help, Mr. Beard."

I was scared to tell her that I hadn't met any patients so far, so I leaned against the door behind me and watched her undress. Constanza Lovesick was ten years older than Mrs. Vegas, with a bit of a belly and hips, which couldn't be ignored in the small room. When she made her first move, I got a fleeting vision of how it would end.

"I hope you don't expect anything too fancy from me, Constanza. Perhaps a quick game of spinning wheel?" I whispered, trying to grope her breasts.

She lit up and said, in a much softer tone, "You are a smart man, Alphonso; you know many things about your kingdom and your women."

It was not hard to find a proper angle to fulfill all her wishes, melding our two bodies as one. I discovered her space fully accommodating, and her yarn-like cave standing guard against any threats from my suddenly awoke fer-de-lance. After a couple of minutes, I lowered my face onto her belly and she tightened her thighs, placing my nose firmly in her grip.

"I've got to get out of here. Wedding, wedding, wife… Where are my clothes?" I was tied to the bed, naked, shaking from the cold.

"In our clinic, when the doctor says you stay, you stay," the round and sweaty face above me replied.

"I have to talk to Mrs. Vegas; it's urgent!" I shouted.

"You are so rude, Alphonso. Do you want to wake up the whole clinic?" Constanza Lovesick wore a professional smile; she began adjusting the ropes on my bed.

"Yes! All fifteen of them!" I tried to escape, but I failed. "Where are they? Hallllooo!! Peeooppple!"

"They are in the jitter room, waiting for their dinner. Our new dietician and cook, Martha SoBeIt, advised to feed them with an extra portion of fresh meat."

"I want my clothes back; it is freezing!" I made the last attempt to flee.

"What for?" a squeaky male voice asked. I looked up only to see Bip SoBeIt's smiling face, standing near the window. He continued, "We simply can't allow you to go outside in this condition, Mr. Beard. I'd never forgive myself if we lost you in our clinic's wild jungle. What if you go out there and get involved in an accident with some mad female patient? We have to keep you safe." He paused. "Yes, this isn't a royal palace. I get it, but it is better than a grave in the local cemetery. Look at the positive side of your situation: you are alive and healthy, and you've got a nice future in our clinic."

"What? What kind of future? I'm the king!" I cried; I was astonished by his power and calmness.

"A fictional king. I'll explain it to you shortly… I just need your signature here and there," Bip SoBeIt said, while throwing a stack of papers in front of my face.

"Does Martha know?" I asked.

"Know what?"

"That you are keeping me here against my will," I screamed. "Maaaarthaaa! Darling!!"

"Ah, don't bother. She is in the backyard; we have a wild party there every Saturday. I think it is terribly romantic, don't you think? A party in the middle of the war and LKED epidemic," Bip SoBeIt laughed. His half-sister echoed him. The horror of that moment enveloped me, and I did the last thing I could ever imagine doing — I started to sing.

insanity of lked

. . .

REMEMBER THE OLD SAYING, "Tough times don't last; Tough people do?" In the next few hours, I confirmed the veracity of these words. I wasn't some kind of mighty hero, but in my head I'd always spun the idea of becoming a new-age Hercules. His personal story resonated with my crazy voyage to Gunung Kinabalu, primarily because of my strength and perseverance to conquer many challenges on the Warrior Farm. I always knew I could behave as a real hero one day.

Naked memories of the sad past covered me against my will. In that lonely moment, I asked the shadow that moved closer and closer, crawling over the damp wall's muddy skin. "You know something? Someday, I'll find her, my Sobekneferu princess. I don't know exactly how or when, but I will. You probably don't believe me, but I can visualize her, like right now, riding out of the clinic on the white horse."

Of course, my poor condition was the reason for that

bizarre statement. But what would happen next—after the tête-à-tête with my soul—was totally out of my craziest expectations.

"I knew guys like you, Mr. Beard… They all ended up dead. At first, I thought it must be some kind of a reaction against me personally, or my latest research." The voice from the corner was familiar. I turned my head to face Alexander Raphael's angry expression. He continued, "But there's a simple, psychiatric explanation. Personally, if you ask me—ah, I know you never will; too busy counting your endless wives. You know what, I think all that dreaming about finding one forever love or a perfect cure is crap. People are so naïve."

"I thought I was a white horse once, too." Mr. FuzzyPie sighed, escaping the sunlight and moving slowly toward my weak body.

I understood the complexity of my situation. That's why I began to rock my bed, unconsciously repeating, "Swim, my boat, swim, my boat, swim," and it did. But not in the direction that I planned. Alexander Raphael and Mr. FuzzyPie grabbed the iron chains and dragged my bed to the window. To tell you honestly, I didn't know what they were up to, and I didn't want to know: ignorance is the only true power in situations like this. The realization that I got a voice came to my rescue. I yelled, "Help! Save your king!"

My ex-wife, Martha, ran into the cell, surrounded by two thugs with massive, brown clubs. During the chaos and fight, my chains somehow fell off, and struggling with pain, all blue, I broke free. In that moment of absolute happiness, somebody hit me from behind. Yes... they just hit me on the head with all their might!

Later, I found out I was not far from the truth. Only thirteen patients—all of them women—were kept inside that clinic. Although, fifteen thousand souls were recorded on the paper for which Mr. SoBeIt and his half-sister, Constanza Lovesick, received money and subsidies from the inhabitants of Gunung Kinabalu and my royal pocket. So, it didn't surprise me when an uprising, which lasted several hours, arose during my stay in captivity.

"Lucky bastard!" were the first words I heard when I opened my eyes. It seems I was still a king, but Alphonso Beard's animated mask was partially smashed.

The thirteen female patients, with their upper bodies uncovered, stood above me with their hair clipped in precisely the same fashion as Alexander Rapahel's hair. They looked so dangerous that I became convinced that it wouldn't matter who I was. They dreamed of killing me without delay. However, seeing that I was unarmed and smiling stupidly, they stood silently and looked at me. Ah, so many thoughts passed through my mind: if only I could've stopped searching for Sobekneferu and given up on trying to be so damn kind to everybody I met!

I felt like I was inside of an illusion because the women around me constantly changed their facial appearances. I understood that that change didn't depend on them but watching their faces twirl like a kaleidoscope made my head spin. I lifted my arms, palms facing forward, and waved like a wizard, feeling foolish and hoping to stop this absurd situation.

"The key to destroying LKED is to wash your souls in bacteriophages and detach yourselves from reality," Alexander Raphael announced, approaching the angry crowd. All thirteen faces jumped up and yelled at the top of their lungs a simple, "Long live the new King Alexander Raphael!"

It made me think they'd won, but the lightning strike from outside the walls somehow hit Mr. Fuzzy-Pie. He fell dead. During the next, much bigger explosion, we retreated to the back of the yard and then out, into the wild jungle behind the clinic's gates.

"My *spindle* is completely stationary. I can't feel it. It looks like it's stopped moving. Can you check it?" I asked the nearest beauty, who helped me to walk upright. Even if she wasn't very comfortable with the idea of checking my *spindle,* she nodded anyway.

"It's hard to explain, but I don't think it is there. Maybe it is gone. Happened to some men I know because the LKED was spreading too fast," the woman explained.

"I thought the LKED disease was only contagious for women?" I stared at her in disbelief.

She answered with a pitiful smile, "No, to all."

Just as I began to wonder how I could use this escape for my personal elevation, I heard a strange conversation.

"We can cast him into the ditch like a dog," one of the women said.

"No, he has to confess all his sins to each family of the Warrior Farm, to all he killed or destroyed."

"Wait! Right, I have a confession to make. It is true: I am not Alphonso Beard. I am Bullet, the harmless one! Remember me?" I shouted.

"You see? A clear sign of madness," whispered the brunette with vast, white teeth into Alexander Raphael's ear.

"Take off this damn mask and you'll see!" I screamed.

Nobody listened. We went off the road to a little field with a sign that read "No trespassing," where the grass grew green and high, where the sun had no power on any side, where the gentle breeze sang about all sunlight and suffering, and where—without any warning—I was cheerfully beaten and hung at the top of the lonely olive tree.

Alexander Raphael and his mad LKED gang opened two bottles of a local alcoholic drink—strong as hell—and gobbled it in a leisurely fashion, celebrating their victory.

"I'm Bullet! Please, I can prove it! Are you going to stay and watch me die? You'll be forever sorry!"

"No. We already know how you'll die," the women laughed.

When the procession left me, a sudden pain began to move through my body: it started in my left eye, then pushed down my neck, arm, and chest, until my already miserable *spindle* was on fire. But as I said earlier, "Tough times don't last; Tough people do." I was on a journey—a very important one. And nothing would stop me.

the jungle revelation

. . .

I KNOW you are wondering why I didn't take advantage of the Gunung Kinabalu Kingdom's opportunities, the Warrior Farm's techniques, or at least sought help from the too-many-to-count assistants that the previous king had. I don't even know what to tell you; the problem was everything happened too fast. I didn't get the opportunity to even think about acquiring some advice or assistance. On the other hand, I was preoccupied with the shining bodies I met along the way—the true stars of this distant land—and I simply couldn't resist their dangerous game. And if I'd tried, my anaconda would have stopped me.

I thought about all that, as well as Margaret, my mother, the hippie captain, and my enemy Arcadio, while hanging upside down on an abandoned piece of the field far beyond the borders of the Warrior Farm. I knew that shouting wouldn't help in any way, so I decided to surrender to the will of fate—I stopped breathing. I thought: *The birds are shitting on me? Why not? They're welcome to! Am I hungry and cold? Whatever. The sooner I die, the better.*

And in the end, I was so resigned to my fate that I wasn't paying attention when Madame Jack approached my tree, coming from nowhere, and began to poke his gross face into my sweaty hair. I shuddered and swung like a pendulum. My whole body began to vibrate from the horrors of what was to come next—getting ready to be eaten by the ugly Madame Jack.

After a couple of minutes, the old rope snapped. My heart stopped: my body fell right on Madame Jack's head, crushing him and turning him into a tiny pancake. I was smeared in his thick greasy blood and hair until I looked like a vampire. Upon closer inspection of his insides, I realized he was a perfectly built biological robot. Despite the terrifying sight of the trampled, burned-out earth around me and a bloody pool under the tree, I somehow brushed myself off, and with my hands still tied behind my back, started to run along the edge of the field, hobbling on one leg, hiding between trees and bushes.

Tormented like a blind puppy, I stumbled into something soft, warm, and pleasant after several hours of exhausting running. My lifeline turned out to be the breasts of my old friend—Ms. Sedative. I know you'll be surprised to hear that. I was surprised just as you are right now, but my silent anaconda lifted its head and whispered, "I'm getting sex-starved here. I could penetrate a wall right now. Couldn't you?"

Odd lustfulness oppressed me. I tried to focus my attention on the ramblings of the worried Ms. Sedative but failed to maintain it. She untied my hands, and they immediately began the process of discovering her silky skin, platinum-colored hips, and confident lips smelling of coffee. An orgasm of fire twisted my heart: it drained the strength out of my body, controlled by my passion. My anaconda transformed my fears into magnificent sensations; despite the emotion of some alien-ness, or better say, the feeling of not belonging with this woman, moment, or journey; I continued our dance on the soggy dirt as a crazy fanatic.

Little by little, I slowed down. I felt curiously disgusted with the darkness my anaconda possessed: a piece of dead flesh, really, the non-existent friend.

"I thought you were dead, Bullet. Does Mrs. Vegas know you are alive?" Ms. Sedative asked.

"I don't know. I have to find the box with the bacteriophages."

"All right. Now? And what then?"

"I'll explain to you later. I want you to go back to my castle and...," I stopped. Ms. Sedative rubbed her perfect hands against my exhausted anaconda.

"I think I'm pregnant."

I pulled her face closer to mine, shocked. "We haven't known each other that long, and I can't get married right now. I'm in the process of marrying Mrs. Vegas; then, I've got one more wife, or widow, Mrs. Sweet Hellfire."

"Um, I wouldn't mind being married to you. And I

don't need to know you for a long time. I know what you're like already, darling Bullet."

"Hm, I dunno about one more wife." I paused for a moment, passed a hand over my wet forehead and wiped my damp fingers on the grass pile behind her back.

Ms. Sedative looked surprised. "You should be more like Arcadio! He always takes an interest in serious questions like this!"

"What? Have you said to that maniac I'm the father?"

"Yes. And Arcadio promised he's going to kill you... I don't know why. I didn't ask him; we were too busy," Ms. Sedative giggled.

I gazed at her pretty face without replying. She glanced behind my back, shook her head, and smiled. At that moment, I could smell the familiar odor of Etro Bananas Tisstoni perfume. Ms. Sedative's crew approached us. The last time I met her gang, it nearly gave me diarrhea. But I'm romantic; I need a real punch in the solar plexus to stop me from feeling excited and ready for action.

"I thought we were alone. What are they doing here?" I asked bitterly.

"We all need friends to lean on. They can help you to find the box."

I accepted the help. I'd stopped wondering whether the girls were good or evil. It didn't matter a damn after the news I'd just gotten. I suddenly felt as if I'd turned into a giant—I was going to be a father! I felt absurdly happy.

While waiting for the ladies to come closer, the new, almost rhapsodical thrill aroused in me again. I smiled at the coral sunset light and spoke in a low voice, "How long does it take them to discover your magic, Bonehead?"

fear

. . .

FOR YEARS *I searched for my home, and I found it only in Gunung Kinabalu: the place of violent but passionate hearts. So, if you'd ask me, after the long journey I took to the Warrior Farm, becoming a doctor and a king was the most satisfying accomplishment in the world and the perfect start for a new life and family.*

I sat beside Ms. Sedative. Our shoulders touched; I could feel the smoothness of her skin. I wanted to tell her how strong she was and how much I admired her from the moment I met her (which would be a lie). I sat, looked at her, and blamed myself for what I'd done to my dreams: I had betrayed the idea of finding my one and only Sobekneferu; I bowed my head submissively before the weak of this world.

Ms. Sedative made an impatient sound. "I already came up with the name—Scleromochlus Pterosauromorpha. What do you think?"

"That's lovely… But it makes me feel dizzy. Can we just call the kid Mochlus or Morpha?"

"No. If you are looking for a shorter name, I propose Ralphie."

"And if it is a girl?" I asked, unsure if I should insist or not.

"Ralphie."

I didn't argue with Ms. Sedative, and I didn't promise her we would call the child Ralphie either. She mistook my silence for an invitation to chat. *Please, somebody, anybody, make her quiet. It's worse than hanging from that tree,* I thought.

"I see you are shaking, Bullet. Get your lil soft bacon in my warming arms," Ms. Sedative chuckled. After those words, I drew away from her as if she'd confessed to having a disease of some sort, got up, and walked over to Holly Terror to check if she was still alive.

Holly was sleeping with her eyes open. I caught a sign of madness in her dreamless face—it worried me. I got more suspicious when I heard Ms. Sedative's ramblings. She was demanding we visit a local cemetery.

"What? Cemeteries are full of dead people," I mumbled. "And we are still alive. The way I see it, my dear... if some of those dead people aren't ready to go, they become ghosts. Do you want to scare your baby's father?"

"Let's pretend we are dead, too. I promise you; they won't notice the difference," Ms. Sedative laughed.

Reasons why I have to leave that child of mine fatherless, soon, very soon, began to multiply in my mind like germs. I turned away from Ms. Sedative and looked at the gang of her mates sitting under the shades of grayness on the empty field in the middle of nowhere.

"Let's go to sleep. An hour in the morning is worth two in the evening," I answered.

Well, you may think I am stupid, and I have to confess that with my IQ of seventy-five, I'm not an intellectual giant, but I just wanted to buy more time before I'd dare to visit a cemetery of the Warrior Farm.

That night, stuffed as a sausage between Candy de Beast's and Ms. Sedative's legs, I dreamed of a little boy trapped in the dirt, unable to get out of the grave. His whole body felt bleak and heavy, stiff with tension. Behind him, I saw my chirping mother, who stroked his head and repeated, "I know the truth. He is not your father, Scleromochlus Pterosauromorpha. He is the old wanky spirit, the demon who wants to destroy your future! Kill him!"

I fled in fear, tripping over rocks and skeletons.

"Would an innocent man have fled like that, Scleromochlus Pterosauromorpha? No way! Get him!" my mother's shadow uttered a sound of disgust.

I don't remember what happened afterward, but in the dream, a toddler jumped on my back, and then Ms. Sedative woke me up, which saved me from being murdered by an angry infant.

"Kids… they are tough," I said. "I'm not sure I can sacrifice my life for one."

"Be careful, Bullet! Scleromochlus Pterosauromorpha can hear you. Some kids grow up and become so sad that all they do for the rest of their lives is run down their poor fathers as prey."

"What if I'm not a father? I can't be a father to such a monster."

"Arcadio said that you are!" she explained as patiently as she could.

I pretended I agreed. Not very professional, I know, but it worked for a couple of minutes. Then I heard a growl behind me: Candy de Beast woke up. Immediately, she pushed me on the grass for a new sexual stretch; as she explained during the process, *it would help her to get the daily hours to pass a little faster*.

She danced naked in front of me, occasionally performing a beautiful pirouette. Her dark hair hung in waves over her shoulders; her body was soft and rounded, built for comfort.

Meanwhile, unhappy and jealous, Ms. Sedative started to change. Her naïve playfulness turned dark; her eyes got more immense. We stood face-to-face, but she wasn't looking at me. She stared at something beyond my left eye as if denying my very presence. Then she slowly put her cold hands on my neck… That was the moment when I knew—the time had come. Run!

But I always hated to run. I never needed to. Still, I convinced myself it was time for an early departure, especially if I'd like to be saved from colliding and being squashed between all five mysterious ladies.

I blinked painfully and opened my eyes. I was still lying in the same spot, in the pool of bloody mess from Madame Jack. Was it only a dream? What if Ms. Sedative was also a biorobot? What if all of them were robots?

between the roads

. . .

MY FATHER ONCE TOLD ME, "When you hit rock bottom, Bullet, there is no place to go but UP."

It's been a difficult time, but I was determined to continue living to the fullest, despite all the pain and horrors of the past hours. That's why I felt proud to stand upright after hanging upside down from the tree. All sorts of thoughts invaded my mind, but each time I came back to one; perhaps the most important: Where's my Sobekneferu? Would I ever find her? Is she dreaming of me as I dream of her? And what is love?

I read somewhere that love, any kind of love, has its stages. It begins with adoration, then turns to longing, and changes slowly to attachment, and finally to a union. You can't even imagine how often I dreamed of it on cold lonely nights in my small studio in Rsa. My mother, instead, always told me that love (any kind and at any stage) was a trap, and that's why she ended up with my spineless, uninspiring, and always-satisfied-with-so-little father—she was deceived, lured into that perfect idyllic union. I played along; an advocate of the "love is a trap" doctrine. In reality, I was *non compos mentis,* and the only sanity was my hope of finding Sobekneferu—the joy, the stream of life, that would push my disastrous sexual experiences upward.

I sighed, turned to the left, and started to walk when I heard a soft splash of water. I hid behind the trees, waiting until the beauty turned her face to the shore. It was the sheriff. She shone in a strange dim light—sole perfection! *Her skin looks too damn good for a woman who's been dead for almost a month,* I said to myself. Her breasts showed zero signs of decomposition, too. At first, I got angry, then frightened, and after a couple of seconds, frustrated. Did it stop me from walking out of my hiding spot when I saw her in the morning light swimming in that lake? No. Hardly. I crawled to the shore (much faster than you'd expect from a damaged man like me); I knew it was the step UP in my arduous journey. I believed it was the moment of establishing contact with the other world (where I was the real human, made of bones and flesh, and she was something else —the beast and fiend). Because of the increased speed and the sand in my eyes, I bumped into the stone and… what do you think? Yes! I dropped into the same pool of blood from Madame Jack, which I had escaped just minutes ago. I got up and slammed my fist in anger on a nearby tree. The pain sobered my senses. I made a brave decision to leave Gunung Kinabalu for good and get back to Rsa—to heal, lick my wounds, and speak with my mother. But destiny, as always, made another decision.

According to the second assistant, Ms. Break de Roof, she found me in an absolute "cuckoo state." I was so scared and shaken that she decided to knock me down again. Then, she hung me in the same spot (and explained she needed more time to think about what to do with me and to determine if I really was Mr. Harmless or some freak from Beluga Clan). She told me later that I spoke of the dead sheriff while unconscious; I even swore I saw her swimming in the lake while she rode a snake and carried a torch, one in each of her six hands.

I was so paranoid that even the wonderful Ms. Break de Roof appeared with three heads: the first was human and pretty; the second belonged to Madam Jack; and the third to the Egyptian ape-headed Thoth. Or, probably, I had psychic abilities and could finally see her true nature?

When I calmed down a little, Ms. Break de Roof informed me of the latest changes in the kingdom: revolution, the division of the territory into two parts, Ms. Vegas's escape, the disappearance of box #9, and the change of the local king and queen. Martha and Mr. Bip SoBeIt ruled a large part of the kingdom now—the so-called Prudent Village; Alexander Raphael got the minor part of the clinic and the territory surrounding it.

I was too tired to listen, so I clung to her feet and folded my trembling hands, repeating, "I want to go home; please, take me home." Her next move was like an apocalypse (I didn't need much at that stage). Ms. Break de Roof smiled and showed me the puffy side of her untrimmed temple. I admit, it touched my heart: I slathered my majestic sword, awaiting a massive ear-splitting attack from the second assistant. Our joyful dance was seen by two passing guards: Medusa and Jellywobble. They tied us up and delivered us to the palace. There, my ex-wife, Martha, dressed in a long gown made of the dead banteng and a crown full of gold needles, announced, "It's my duty as Queen of The Prudent Village to caution you, Mr. Harmless. Our new laws forbid sexual encounters outside of the house."

"What?"

"Our new laws treat stealing bacteriophages as a severe crime, too. If you tell me privately where you hid box #9, I'll let you live, Mr. Harmless."

"Good heavens! Martha, it's me… your ex-husband, Bullet. What's the…?"

"My name is Martha Antoinette Louise Diamantis SoBeIt! And by the law of the Prudent Village, you should…," my ex-wife yelled.

"Okay, okay, Martha Antoinette Louise Diamantis SoBeIt, whatever… I don't have it. Put it in capital letters if you wish! To steal is not my style at all. And you know me, I am an honest man."

"You have the time to find it," she paused. "Until 4:00 this afternoon."

"What time is it now?" I asked impatiently.

"Three-fifty-eight. Time is ticking… What are you waiting for? Go!"

I saw a tall, bearded man in a long white robe at the other end of the room. He began to sing a prayer in a high-pitched voice. I tried to hide under the dining table, behind curtains, and in the bathtub, but nothing helped. The clock struck three-fifty-nine. I dove through the iron door, rushed along the wet corridor, and ran into the room, which, as it turned out, was the Royal Kitchen. An almost invisible silhouette leaned over a huge saucepan and stirred something with a wooden spoon. On the table, by a saucepan, stood box #9. A sigh of relief left my chest… and then the clock struck 4.00.

in the kitchen

. . .

FOR EVERY ACCIDENT IN LIFE, *there are many different angles from which to view it. When I look back now at the events of that day in the kitchen, I see it from a wider perspective, with a greater joy. But back then…*

A dish full of exquisite flavors and texture gurgled in a copper saucepan. While I enjoyed the unfamiliar aroma, a woman of the futuristic, almost geometric shape in a plush hat—Miss Downhill Tasty—took box #9 from the table and threw it into the saucepan without looking at it or opening it. I observed how she roughly chopped the hazelnuts and blackberries and peeled an ostrich-like mosquito (perhaps a genetic manipulation) that could have weighed several kilograms, setting the raw spices aside in separate bowls.

"Are you mad? What have you done? That was the box with bacteriophages," I sobbed. "You just murdered me, my hopes to meet Sobekneferu, and my future."

"Mr. Bip SoBelt loves some soap in his dishes. It cleanses the body, he says. And it gives an extra moisturizer for the brain." Miss Downhill Tasty paused. "The box was empty when I got it."

The clock struck 4.00 again. It didn't alert me, although it should have. I was stunned—I stood in the middle of the room and watched the cook's skeletal hands with doubt and suspicion.

"Why are you looking at me like that?" she asked.

"I'm just thinking…"

"That's not a reason to stare, Mr. Harmless."

"It's reason enough for anything!"

I grabbed her from behind, swooped her up in my arms, and carried her to the chair near the window. There I pressed my lips against her neck's cold, moist skin and shook her like an aspen tree. I began to suspect that my wild actions pleased her as she moaned—somewhat inspiringly, reverently, with a whistle and softness. She didn't stop, so I swayed her more and more.

"Yes, yes, yeees!" she whispered.

"Shh, I'll continue if you tell me where you got this box," I winked. "Tell me, and I'll rock you as much as you want on my magic wand; it will be like a carousel. I promise."

"There was nothing inside, only the soap. Mrs. Cactus handed it to me and said I could do whatever I want with the box," Ms. Downhill Tasty replied.

"Aha!" I exclaimed and pushed the cook away with such force that she flew off to the door and crashed into the incoming Martha.

"It is 4:00 and thirty-eight seconds," Martha announced. "Where is box #9?"

"Here. Inside of this soup, my dear Martha

Antoinette Louise Diamantis SoBeIt!" I bowed gallantly, pointing at the boiling saucepan with protruding wings and huge claws.

Martha groaned and ran around the stove. She tried to cool down the contents of the soup and take out box #9. I grabbed the dumbfounded cook, pressed her closer, and whispered, "One more question. Where can I find Mrs. Cactus?"

"I won't tell. You promised a carousel and a magic wand, and what have I gotten? Only bruises," Ms. Downhill Tasty whispered back.

"I am a dead man! Do you want to use a dead man's wand and ride a broken carousel?" I hissed.

The cook pouted her lips and turned her face to the wall. I decided to drop my pants to free my angry animal. The air around me thickened, and the whole room disappeared—the pans and stove were no more than dim and dirty halos. Ms. Downhill Tasty shut her eyes and braced her tiny being against me. She gasped and uttered a long, guttural roar, trashing the air in my mouth with her forked tongue. Of course, I accepted her non-verbal request—I knew she was ready to welcome my demonic seeds.

During our inspiring and heated conversation, I learned about the secret passage behind the curtains in the bedroom of the now-deceased Alphonso Beard. It turned out the tunnel led straight to Mrs. Cactus's bedroom, and she did not hesitate to use it each time she wanted to visit the previous king.

"Of course! How could I forget?!" I hit myself on the forehead and ran out of the kitchen without pulling up my pants, which frightened Mr. SoBeIt, who, with sleepy eyes, went out to the hall to see what had caused such a horrible noise. I ran past him into the bedroom, behind the curtain, rolled down the steps, and dropped at a luxurious sofa upholstered in yellow silk. A pure goddess was lying on it. The time struck 4.01.

"Sobek…ne-fe-rruu?" I stuttered.

"Hello, Mr. Harmless! You can call me whatever you want, but just a day ago, I was Mrs. Cactus."

"It's im-pos-si-ble!" I choked with delight.

"Everything is possible in the Rejuvenate Center of the West Palace. They do wonders with tired people like me," she glowed and glanced at my bruised legs. "What do you want? Why the rush? I'm in the middle of a painting session. I hired famous painters from different parts of the world to create a new, fresh portrait of me."

After her comment, I noticed twelve pairs of surprised eyes staring up at us with brushes in their hands.

"I need to know where the bacteriophages are from box #9," I said.

"Where? You're looking at them, Bullet! How do you think I made this perfect new body and face? I sold them to Beluga Clan," The woman laughed.

The clock struck 4.02. I realized that this was the end —I was two minutes late, and the bacteriophages were gone forever. But as T.S. Elliot once said, "The end is where we start from."

between life and death

. . .

WHEN THE BAG was removed from my head, the first thing that caught my eye was a chain of long tables with hundreds of people sitting in companionable silence. Most of them were rocking back and forth as if in a trance.

"What's up?" I asked cheerfully. My hoarse voice scared a young man on the bench closest to the door. He sunk down to the floor on all fours and crawled on his stomach to the wall. To say I was shocked by his behavior would be an understatement.

I was still recovering from this strange incident when a heavy hand patted me on my left shoulder. The hand belonged to Constanza Lovesick. I jumped up, alerted by her compassionate action.

"Sorry," she bit her lip. "I thought I imagined things. It couldn't be Bullet, I said to myself. But here you are."

"Yes, here I am, alive and transcending positivity of the highest level."

"What do you mean?"

"I mean a) I don't understand how I got here, b) nobody warned me about this place, and c) why hang around and feel like a sucker or complain about how unfair life is when the room is full of beautiful people such as yourself, Constanza." I touched her soft cheeks and added, "You and I could transform this room together."

"How?"

"There are tons of possibilities!"

"But everybody in this bunker will play a part in creating the dessert for the banquet in honor of the Beluga Clan's victory yesterday."

"Okay. Then, what is the tragedy?"

"Well, that means we are food."

Constanza Lovesick explained that our room was like a storage cellar full of the best ingredients for the weekly celebrations. Those who couldn't be honored to be a part of the dish (because of health status) would be sent to the Slave Market in the Back-Block Province. When I asked Constanza Lovesick how she got here, she only sobbed.

I wasn't ready to give up. I started to walk around the tables and began to think in hopes of finding a solution.

Two desires—two invisible wings—raise our human spirit above everything else: the desire to live and the desire for the truth. We naturally want to live forever, but the laws of our universe (or Mother Nature) do not permit eternal life. This knowledge leaves us abandoned, but with a burning desire to achieve immortality one day.

We crave the truth from others but often forget about

ourselves. The voice of selfishness points out our daily (sometimes, very small) lies, which does not allow us to live in the complete truth, as this can lead to premature death, especially in places like the Warrior Farm or Beluga Clan. Thus, lies keep us in its jaws, offering us a carefree life in return, but slowly—drop-by-drop. And we are happy. We accept it. But if there is no real, true us, then there will be no life and there will be no one and nothing to learn, build, or love. There will be no evil and no truth. Even the need for the ego will disappear… hm. I don't know about you, but I'd like to continue to live, and I'd lie with great joy if I had to. My desire to live is much stronger than my desire for truth!

I stopped running in circles and whispered through my teeth, "Animals! I refuse to be someone's food!"

"What can we do? The reason humanity exists is food, but the *purpose* of our existence is reproduction," remarked an old man with gray whiskers at the other end of the table. And then it dawned on me—of course, reproduction. Maybe I could still save myself from an early death of becoming some collagen additive in a dessert served to the monsters of the Beluga Clan. I decided to offer my *anaconda's skills* in exchange for my freedom. With that in mind, I jumped on the bench and yelled with all my might, "What are we living for, people? What is the purpose of our lives?"

"Look at this damn philosopher; shut up already," a hundred voices hissed from all sides.

A naïve part of me continued to yell, "Listen to your nature! What is your nature asking for? For love! Let's make love!"

Four firm hands interrupted my performance,

dragged my resisting body out of the room, and threw me into a dark dungeon. The cell was filled with a strange liquid—some kind of marinade. Beethoven's *Moonlight Sonata* played from the speaker in the corner. A deep nostalgia for the Warrior Farm and regret for being such a bad doctor to the women with LKED problems washed over me like a wave. I understood, Beluga Clan had made their decision: I'm going to die.

Tears rolled down from my eyes. My short journey in search of Sobekneferu ended in the realm of death. But I did not want to die alone. In that second, I made a promise to myself: before I die, I'll take at least one villain from the Beluga Clan with me to the world of the Duat. Moans, sobs, and howls from neighboring cells convinced me that the only way to gain salvation was through murder—the only proper punishment for the wicked. You know me, you've followed me on my journey. You understand I didn't want to kill anyone, but the laws of this country had created a demon-like creature and I was ready to fight for my life.

I was hungry and thirsty, so I began my confrontation by sipping salty water in the room, and in the end, I drank so much that there was nothing left.

The door opened, and a husky female voice asked, "Are you Harmless, famous heavy weightlifter from Rsa?"

"Whaaat?" I hiccupped.

"Ms. Glorious sent me... She told my brother, commander in chief of our army, that you were famous in the Rsa because you could lift anything you wanted."

"Am I?"

"Where's the marinade?" The pretty female guard looked perplexed.

"I hid it."

"Wow… How? What are you, Mister?"

"I am, my darling girl, a magician. I can lift or hide anything I want. Would you like to take part in an experiment?"

"Of course," she said, smiling.

I smiled back and put my hands on her waist. At that moment, someone spat on my back. The same person kicked me in the leg with a metallic boot and said, "Nice move, pigeon."

I turned around to see my opponent. Above me stood a cyborg woman dressed in a man's suit with a long silver whip in her hand. She muttered something through her teeth and spat again, this time on my bare chest. The other female guard ran out of the room and left me alone with the malicious beast.

"Mr. Vegas would like a quick chat," the female cyborg said.

"M-m-mister?"

"Yes."

"You must be mistaken, my lovely lady," I reached out to touch my enemy in the narrow damp hall.

"Shut up and walk ahead; otherwise, I'll have to gag you."

"Please do because I refuse to follow your orders, Miss… umm, what's your name?"

"Sobekneferu," the cyborg replied and spat again.

O, Destiny, why are you so cruel to me?!

sobekneferu

. . .

I TRIED *to convince myself that female cyborgs were cute. Who cares that she looked like a nuclear mutant? I'd still spend a few genuinely jolly minutes in her arms if it saved me from meeting with Mr. Vegas.*

"Do you want to know a secret?" I asked the cyborg, trying to slow her down. "I am a divine magnet for women with the name Sobekneferu."

"All right, Magnet… Turn right and follow me."

I don't recall how we ended up near stone-carved doors. When they opened, I saw an extraordinary vehicle waiting for us outside, a sort of car-plane hybrid. The fog thickened; I couldn't see my arms. But the bad weather didn't stop Sobekneferu from pushing me inside the strange device. We took off and quickly accelerated, the cyborg's hands gripped the steering wheel so tightly that the cells in my brain ached.

I must stay calm if I'm going to deal with this crazy female gadget, I thought while analyzing Sobekneferu's face. She stared into nowhere like a mathematician faced with a complex equation. Five minutes later, she announced, "We've arrived."

Knowing I was about to meet Mr. Vegas upset me, but it was better than becoming someone's dinner or being locked up for life in prison. I made a quick decision to behave according to the situation.

"What are you mumbling there? Get your arse out, Magnet," Sobekneferu ordered.

I stepped out carefully and looked across the darkness to the scattered lights glittering through the mist somewhere far away.

"Where are we?" I asked.

"This is your home for the next few weeks," Sobekneferu explained.

I heard a noise behind me and turned to face it. There, just a few meters away, stood the most peculiar creature I'd ever seen—a giant black honeybee—and it was moving towards me. I remember wondering if I was dreaming, or perhaps I'd become a hero in Kafka's cautionary tale.

"Hello, Xenophon. Look what I've brought—a new *hick* to your camp," Sobekneferu said.

"What's his name?" asked the buffy creature.

"I call him Pigeon. He calls himself Magnet."

Here my story takes an unexpected turn. Behind Xenophon, stood Arcadio. What's more peculiar, when the Sobekneferu-cyborg saw him, she ran to him, fell to her knees, and hugged his feet.

"Look at you, Bullet! You are still alive," Arcadio chuckled, ignoring the robot's body on the ground in front of him. "Well, I'm here to inform you that Mr.

Vegas had to leave Beluga Clan in a rush… some family troubles if I understood correctly. I spoke with him before his departure, and we decided to give you a chance to live, at least for now. I doubt anyone can survive more than two weeks inside The Slave Market."

"If only you would stop navel-gazing for a second, you'd see that I'm not your enemy, Arcadio. And we aren't that different, after all."

"Oh, I know. I just simply don't like you, Bullet!"

"That's fine. Perhaps one day you'll change your mind… and you know what, Arcadio? I like you anyway," I lied.

"You are not supposed to like someone who doesn't like you. Don't you see? That's why I hate you, Bullet. You don't have a spine; you are always trying to behave according to the situation you are in. Or maybe you really are that stupid." Arcadio hesitated a moment, then laughed. The harsh laugh of a cyborg followed him. It was like a signal from an animal that couldn't communicate in words but wanted to draw attention to itself.

"Hello! Who are you? Hm, I've seen your face before," Xenophon took one step closer to me.

"What's the matter with you?" I squealed.

"I forgot to mention, Xenophon is not capable of remembering faces. But he can relate to what he is seeing. So, please, make him feel good. It's in your best interest," Arcadio said.

That was truly frightening information. As a result, I started to twitch from side to side like a tumbler. In an attempt to calm me down, Xenophon hugged me and held me in his cauliflower-sized arms for a couple of seconds. The hug improved our relationship, but I was smeared with some kind of black soot and became just as dirty and frightening as Xenophon himself.

"Everything's going to be okay. Things will work out one way or another," I whispered calmly. I tried to convince myself that I was one of those who kept moving forward with little complaint and plenty of competence, but then Sobekneferu—still sitting near Arcadio's feet—asked, "Shouldn't we replace or shackle his *stick*?"

Arcadio lit a cigarette and blew the smoke out of his mouth before answering, "Yes, true. It's an old rule."

When I heard the news, I lost my ability to speak. It was worse than facing the wrath of the powerful Mr. Vegas. I glanced hatefully at happy Arcadio (the feeling was mutual).

"You can't do that!" I shook my head and cried. "I thought you were sane and reasonable people here in Beluga Clan, but I was clearly wrong."

Xenophon didn't listen; he tied me up. Sobekneferu-cyborg's cold hands pushed my sad *spindle* inside the heavy granite sock specifically designed for people living in the Slave Market. This horrible experience left me with a profound philosophical question: what is the meaning of life if you can't use your superior power of love?

"If you find a partner, the problem may be compounded," Xenophon hummed in my ear.

That information inspired me to jump up and shout like a maniac, "Sobekneferu! I want Sobekneferu!"

I knew I couldn't name Mrs. Sweet Hellfire because she was too far away, and I hadn't been able to marry Mrs. Vegas yet, because of all that awful business at the Clinic, so a female cyborg was my only chance.

"Sobekneferu is my second fiancée... If you want to get rid of that sock, I suggest you marry Xenophon," Arcadio chuckled.

"I can't," I remarked sarcastically. "He has a brain the size of the letter 'o.'"

"Really? The person you have chosen as your partner is unlikely to be any smarter than you are. As I see it, you and Xenophon are a perfect match!"

"Wait...," I said to Arcadio, who had suddenly lost all interest in me. "I have another woman in mind. Her name is Constanza Lovesick. She is the one I'm choosing as my partner! We had such a good connection at the Warrior Farm and started a wonderfully intimate dialogue in the clinic."

"Okay. We got it... I'll bring Constanza Lovesick down," Sobekneferu nodded to Xenophon and followed Arcadio into the darkness. I heard the engine humming far away; the plane took off, leaving me alone with Xenophon. Something wet and heavy touched my leg. I turned around and found myself standing in a hole in the dirt.

"What's going on?" I asked.

"Just trying to find the door. This is where we really live, in an underground complex called Nemesis, right beneath the Beluga's land," the dark shadow of Xenophon answered.

"Okay, but don't we have to wait for Constanza's arrival?"

"To hell with it. There's plenty of time down there!" Xenophon laughed and forced me to jump. I landed on all fours. The room was gloomy and sticky, with a twisting green staircase. I blinked several times, unsure of what to do next.

"Here's what's going to happen now, boy. You and I are going to live together. I have a daughter, Geraldine, who is a very needy child," Xenophon explained.

"How old is she?" I asked, shivering.

"Mmm… Just as you are."

"Why not? Easy peasy," I joked, then closed my eyes and imagined a sweet, round lady with a heart of gold.

"Don't 'easy peasy' me. Let's go; we have to get a present for her." Xenophon's reply interrupted my foolish dreams.

"What kind of present?"

"Some kind of worm that lives in rats' hair," Xenophon explained. I winced in disgust but hobbled after his hairy silhouette.

Two hours later, we sat in a big room without windows. Xenophon's daughter, Geraldine DribbDrobb—a six-foot tall female with a double chin and tiny lips—ran in and pressed me against the wall. Her eyes radiated with lust and hunger.

"I always get a little breathless when I meet a new husband," she squeaked.

"How many have you had?" I asked.

"Not so many… seventy, or nearly eighty in the past

week," Xenophon answered, presenting a bottle of worms placed on a yellow tray.

"Ah, Papa… my Miss Sobekneferu is gonna love it!" Geraldine yelled.

"Who is Miss Sobe-kne-ff-feru?" I coughed, shocked and hopeful at the same time.

"You'll see soon enough," Geraldine winked.

What if I meet my one and only Sobekneferu here? And what if Geraldine looks different tomorrow, in daylight? I thought to myself while following her upstairs. Moments later, I felt a sting in my neck and the cold sensation that came with an injection. Everything began to swirl…

i've seen that face before

. . .

"WAKE UP!" someone shouted louder this time. "You have the power to conquer whatever comes your way. Nothing can stop you!"

I tried to turn left and right — it was useless: my shoulders were stuck in some kind of alabaster, my lips were sealed with duct tape, and my legs were placed in a metal box with a huge padlock, turning me into an odd sculpture. My eyes were not covered, just like hundreds of others in the vast, cold hall. How did I get here?

A half-hour later (after counting all the flies on the walls), as I began to think that the room I'd been placed in was the most beautiful place in the world, the glass door above me opened, and a ray of sun blinded me. I shut my eyes and focused on the sights, smells, sounds, thoughts, and voila — I recalled what had happened to me in the last 24 hours.

Before

I was lying in Geraldine's room, on the bed covered in white flowers. I was paralyzed by some kind of poison but could still hear each word and movement. I listened to Xenophon's daughter, she was standing in the dark corner, speaking with a flowerpot.

"I begged my father to get me the finest worms for you, Sobi... but you know men. Do they know anything about nurturing or beauty?" She sighed. Two withered buds swayed in agreement. "Have I ever not provided a special gift for the birthday of Mrs. Fabulous-Corkscrew? I have a perfect gift this year if not the best offering..." The mumbling stopped. Ms. Geraldine DribbDrobb seemed to have fallen into a coma.

I waited. Nothing happened. The woman started to snore. I moved a finger – the poison was beginning to wear off.

"Mr. Harmless, you are a bad, bad man, " Geraldine said softly. Her eyes, still blurred, were staring at the wall before her. Then she glanced over her shoulder at the table where I struggled with the padlock.

"I think we need more flowers. Piles and piles of flowers!" Ms. Geraldine DribbDrobb clapped her hands and laughed. "I don't know if I can get that many until tomorrow... During the last celebration, we used all the flowers in the Nemesis!" I shook my head and mumbled, "Please, no more," but she didn't pay attention and continued her weird conversation with a flower. "What are you trying to say, darling Sobi? Ah, I get it, don't you worry... Of course, you are right; real flesh and bones is always better than those artificial worms that Daddy gets you."

I groaned. Geraldine's voice changed: "Do you hear it, Sobekneferu? Yes, he is the one. I feel it. His is going to make you happy. You, him, and the soil of Nemesis — all three united..." She rolled her eyes and made a frightening sound of satisfaction and pleasure.

The rest of the time passed slowly. In the end, Geraldine got tired of my ridiculous communication attempts and finally left me alone with my thoughts.

Now, I'd like to mention that the women of the Slave Market were not evil; rather, they were both good and evil, like nature itself. They were social creatures during the day, which I noted early on. As the shadows of Erebus — the ancient deity of darkness — descended on the Nemesis, each of them, depending on the mood, slowly transformed into the irrational Calypso, or faceless Venus of Willendorf, or ritualistic Eve. The female and the serpent, all in one, wandering the Underworld of this Earth in search of the satisfaction of her desires — craving and despising, but never content. The true metamorphosis of nature... that's who they were in my eyes. And yes, I couldn't understand them for a long time. One moment, they'd cry on my shoulder, and the next, they'd scratch my eyes out. There was never a second of peace in the house of Geraldine DribbDrobb. Women came in, touched my sculptured body, drank herbal tea, and then... left. No one tried to get a better look at my brilliant Hercules. What a shame!

When her father, Xenophon, opened the door, I wasn't too excited because I knew he hadn't come to set me free from the claws of his daughter. I watched how he slid up to the middle of the room, bent down, and whispered into my ear: "I've been waiting till I could talk to you alone, Magnet. I've got a message for you from Mrs. Vegas the Fifth."

"What does she say?" I rejoiced; my heart shouted in silence.

"She begs you to accept your fate. She begs you to stay in the Tomb tomorrow. I mean, I hope you know they'll leave you in the Tomb after the ceremony, usually one hour before sunset." Xenophon sighed. "Please, don't try to be a hero and plan an escape. You must stay there. That was her message."

Xenophon glided away before I could come up with any kind of answer. My mood worsened. I felt awful at the prospect of going to some sort of tomb and waiting for my doom. The only thing that lightened up my spirit was that Mrs. Vegas remembered me (and she helped me before): she probably risked her life to send me that message into a world she wasn't familiar with. And it meant a lot.

I heard a surprised moan, then a blow as one more body was placed on the floor. It was covered in a dirty linen sheet. Geraldine DribbDrobb winked at me, her eyes full of intrigue, and left the room again. I hoped the body on the floor was Constanza Lovesick, but to my surprise, it belonged to an unknown male — I recognized a sticking-out sock of granite. I turned to the left because I wanted to see the face of my fellow sufferer, but someone pasted a thick black fabric over his face, leaving only two small holes for the eyes.

I had a dream last night that I was with my one and only Sobekneferu: the Queen of my world. She was standing above me, her floral dress fluttered in the wind, her perfect hand made an invisible wave, and the ground under our feet started to move. Our beautiful boat sailed into the sunrise. I felt happy. I was saved.

"Time to go, Magnet..." Xenophon whispered. "Geraldine, why does he look so strange? Maybe we should feed him?"

"Let us be honest, Papa... He is a part of our 'Law and Order Sacrifice.' He upset Mr. Vegas and his lovely mother all the time. He is simply a dangerous man. A bad, mad man... To send him to the Tomb is the right thing to do," Geraldine replied.

Xenophon interrupted her: "You are right. I remember I was slightly afraid of him when I first met him."

"You see? My dear Papa, do not mourn him."

At that moment, Xenophon grabbed my legs and dragged my weak body down. There, outside of his house, stood a long procession of silent and sad people. Many of them pulled a body or two behind them. After a short walk, we arrived near a long black tunnel. Above, I noticed a sign that scared me more than Xenophon's relatives. It read: "The Place of No Return." *Such an inscription could inspire some heroic deeds,* I thought to myself. Still, when a yellow-faced old man with a long beard, thick eyebrows, and a bare, knobby skull with the horns of a bull crawled out of the gates of the tunnel and began to lament about the frailty of our existence, about the thirst for love as the root of all suffering, about the purification of the world and the wisdom of Beluga Clan rulers, I decided to wait and see what happens next. His preaching did little to enliven the crowd of tired people who listened and continued to drag the bodies inside his tunnel. Xenophon followed.

All I remember about the tunnel was that 1) it was wet and chilly; 2) Geraldine DribbDrobb shook like an animal coming out of the water, sniffed the air inside the tunnel, ran around us, and cursed.

I wanted to die, but a firm hand pulled me into the bright light. In an instant, I knew that something frightening was on the way. I had detected the scent of fear even from the witch-like Geraldine DribbDrobb. When my eyes got used to the blinding light, I saw that I was one of many figurines standing in the big room painted white with a glass door above us. The glass door opened, and an eagle with six wings flew down. I wanted to ask the yellow-faced old man what that eagle represents, but only a weak moan came from my granite abode. But the old man understood my wish; he jumped onto the empty pedestal in the middle of the room and shouted: "Do you wanna ask the Bird Eye in the Sky where he comes from, where he goes, and why?"

I nodded and focused on listening to his answer, but the insects inside of the alabaster (they made a tiny but sharp carcass-house near my testicles) went berserk and bit my *anaconda* with such strength it made me cry out in vain as no one heard, saw or noticed anything.

The eagle collapsed on the ground where a happy Geraldine DribbDrobb unrolled a red carpet.

"Mrs. FabulousCorkscrew would like to meet you all now," Geraldine announced proudly.

My shaft and testicles burned as I was fired at with three hundred tiny, ravenous bullets, but I tried to stay focused. I wanted to meet my enemy face to face.

"I'd like to have a little appetizer first…" a familiar voice said. I looked up. It was a woman I knew too well. It was my mother.

Now

"If you can eat them, beat them! This is what Mr. Vegas told me yesterday. Or maybe it was vice versa; I'm not sure anymore." My mother smiled and patted a yellow-faced old man on the back. "Are they all here? As we discussed?"

She wore a red dress with a huge shining train that stretched down the stairs. I heard the distant steps, and a few minutes later, a strong figure of a man with a springy, confident gait appeared before me. To my surprise, the man was a psychiatrist, Mr. Brahman-Carrado.

"We are ready for the explosion, Ma'am. It will kill the weakest population; the strongest will survive and continue their service for our Clan as usual. Or even better."

My mother raised her finger and said thoughtfully with emphasis, "Beluga Clan need only the strongest slaves. Do not forget about our plan to conquer the world. And I'm not talking here about some Warrior Farm or Rsa… I mean THE WHOLE WORLD!"

Mr. Brahman-Carrado grinned, then got down on his knee and kissed the hem of the woman's train. He whispered from the floor, "What about your son, Bullet? I think he is here."

"A son? Ah, please… that weak bastard? I never had a son. He was adopted."

Mr. Brahman-Carrado smiled and pressed the small button in his hand. The repetitive knocking and vibrations transformed my spine into a bow, my eyes shrank to the size of coarse-ground peppers, and my hair started to dance on its own. Most probably, I was dead…

author's note

This is not the end. It is not even the beginning of the end. Or perhaps, this is the end of the beginning. The story of Bullet continues in the next book, "Bullet's Adventure: Beluga Clan."

www.ingramcontent.com/pod-product-compliance
Lightning Source LLC
LaVergne TN
LVHW012049160826
845678LV00014B/2760

* 9 7 8 9 1 9 8 5 6 0 2 1 3 *